Psychodrama:
Experience and Process

Elaine Eller Goldman
Delcy Schram Morrison

Camelback Hospitals
Western Institute for Psychodrama

**KENDALL/HUNT
PUBLISHING COMPANY**
Dubuque, Iowa

Copyright © 1984 by Kendall/Hunt Publishing Company

Library of Congress Catalog Card Number: 84–81184

ISBN 0–8403–3322–6

Printed in the United States of America

B   403322   01

Contents

Our patients have taught us much about the human spirit—the ways that people can survive in spite of "man's inhumanity to man." Our students have challenged us to find newer, clearer ways to teach. It is to those people, the patients and the students, that we dedicate this book.

Foreword

It was with great pleasure that I accepted the authors' invitation to write a Foreword to this volume. I claim no expertise in psychodrama as a psychodramatist; however, it has been my good fortune to clinically observe the benefits afforded by this psychotherapeutic technique to inpatients and outpatients over the past several years. During this time I have felt it would be a fruitful development to set forth the manner in which classic psychodrama demonstrates, clarifies and helps resolve the core conflicts that patients with a variety of psychiatric conditions present when seeking treatment.

A glance at the table of contents will indicate the range covered by the authors' examination of the interrelation and interaction between the various psychiatric disorders and the role psychodrama can play in the total treatment of patients.

Psychotherapeutic processes are frequently misunderstood and not as easily observed as "medical" treatment models. In "Psychodrama: Experience and Process", the reader can learn the portions, terminology, process, and come close to experiencing the session and its attendant feelings. Thus, this book is helpful for all therapists in learning, in a cogent fashion, about psychodrama techniques. Furthermore, an appreciation of earlier training in theories of human behavior, its development and its aberrations, is enhanced by becoming familiar with the illuminating and synthesizing abilities of psychodrama.

Finally, the process described in this book reminds all of us of the universality of human feelings, experiences, perceptions and distresses. Our sensibility is heightened, once again, to those things we all share. Consequently, our therapeutic effectiveness is enhanced.

In all, I feel that "Psychodrama: Experience and Process" will enjoy success and offer all mental health professionals a most helpful explanation of this particular treatment process and how it complements other therapeutic interventions for the ultimate benefit of those seeking our help.

Phoenix Camelback Hospital
Phoenix, Arizona 1984

Howard S. Gray, M.D.
Medical Director

Acknowledgments

We wish to acknowledge these "significant others" for their encouragement in this endeavor.

William Talmadge Scott, Jr. for the spiral diagrams; Sally Ann Scott, MSW for her editorial assistance; Mark Steven Goldman for the photographs and his on-going assistance; Zerka T. Moreno for permission to use her article and for her influence on our work; Irene Andrie, our hospital administrator, for her continued support in all of our projects.

and

In fond memory of Howard S. Gray, M.D.
1935–1984

Introduction

Today's world is saturated with anger, tension and violence. Little value is placed on human life, responsibility and dignity. We are in need of some means of challenging that violence and of promoting understanding between human beings. Psychodrama, a method of group psychotherapy and one of the most substantial advances in therapy in this century has the potential to produce that understanding and reciprocal accountability.

The basic concepts of Psychodrama, Sociometry and Group Psychotherapy were conceived by Jacob Levy Moreno, M.D. Moreno was born in Bucharest in 1890, but soon moved with his family to Vienna. As a young medical student, Moreno, possessed of a poetic imagination, spent much of his time in the parks of Vienna where children became his first "psychodramatic subjects." Watching the children with their parents and nurses, he decided they needed a special teacher, and he appointed himself. Gathering groups of children around him, he would spin wondrous fairy tales that captured their imaginations. He reported that they were soon spontaneously enacting myths and stories of their own and in the process getting rid of some of their hostility.[1]

The concept of drama as therapy evolved from an experiment Moreno launched in Vienna after World War I, called the "Theatre of Spontaneity." Moreno's Theatre of Spontaneity in 1921 became the basis for his "Theatre of Psychodrama."[2]

Early in his medical career Moreno was put in charge of a refugee camp at Mittendorf, near Vienna. It was here, while watching the plight of the displaced persons, heightened by psychological tensions, that he developed the ideas for the sociometric structures of groups. It was here that he began the basis for his therapeutic method, the concept of role reversal, the existential "meeting eye to eye," the "exchange of eyes" so that an individual might see with the eyes of the "other."[3]

> "A meeting of two:
> eye to eye, face to face.
> And when you are near
> I will tear your eyes out
> and place them instead of mine,

and you will tear my eyes out
and will place them instead of yours,
then I will look at you with your eyes
and you will look at me with mine.[4]

Moreno emigrated to the United States in 1925. His research and findings over the years became the basis of group therapy methods. In particular, Psychodrama and Sociometry were used in hospitals, reform institutes, prisons and schools. Acceptance to Moreno's ideas was slow. The influential Freudians disliked his theories as well as his showmanship.

It is difficult to present comparative evaluations of Moreno's methods because they are so completely existential. However, the American Psychiatric Association elected him a member, and psychiatric hospitals, schools and institutions throughout the world are now accepting the value and power of psychodrama.

According to a study by John Mann of New York University, forty-one studies have substantiated that fundamental changes in behavior take place when psychodrama is used.[5] Dr. Lewis Yablonsky, in a study of drug addicts taken over a three year period, has proven psychodrama effective with one-hundred-fifty individuals who encountered complete failure with other methods of treatment.[6] In working with three-hundred alcoholics over a period of four years, Hannah B. Weiner states, ". . . psychodrama, above all, challenges the alcoholic into action and stops him from becoming a spectator to his autotelic moving pictures of life, into a dynamic adventure in living."[7]

Using the application of Moreno's spontaneity training with institutionalized mental retardates, researchers have concluded that morons can be stimulated in social situations in an intelligent manner.[8] In another study, simple situations were outlined for role playing by individuals whose I.Q.'s ranged from 50–84. The retardates enriched their experiences and gained valuable insight into the feelings and emotions of others. They also learned to employ imagination, interpretation, analysis and reconstruction.[9]

In a book published in England entitled, Please Can I Play God ?, the author, a young school teacher in the London slums, tells of her success in reaching the children with psychodrama, of developing their spontaneity and creativity and enriching their lives in the process.[10]

The term "psyche" is defined as the mind—the mental life of an individual comprising the intellectual, emotional and impulsive activities."Drama" is a transliteration of the Greek word which means action, or a thing done. Therefore, Moreno defined psychodrama as the science which explores the human psyche through dramatic action. "One of its objectives is to teach people to resolve their conflicts in a microcosm of the world (the group) free of conventional restraints, by acting out their problems, ambitions, dreams and fears. It emphasizes maximum involvement with others, investigating conflicts in their immediate and present form in addition to dealing with the subject's early memories and perceptions."[11]

There are many volumes in print that delineate more fully the historical background and the development of the psychodrama movement. These range from the books by Moreno himself, beginning as early as 1914, on to the present output by many of Moreno's students and disciples. We are students of Moreno, teachers of his work; and have always given full credit to his incredible mind and all of its creations. Particularly those methods that are contained in the triadic concept of Psychodrama, Sociometry and Group Psychotherapy. Therefore, we have chosen to exclude the detailed historical perspective and the development of all of his other seminal work, and to focus primarily on the method of psychodrama. We will discuss the process, the form and shape of the session and the creativity of this powerful therapeutic tool.

This book is specifically for the professional practitioner—for the psychodramatist, the student and/or group therapist—to understand the classic, complete, protagonist centered psychodrama. Psychodrama is not incomprehensible or mystical, nor is it a group of techniques to be used at will. More correctly, it is an extraordinary and potent method that can bring insight, catharsis, integration and change in human behavior when understood clearly and used properly. One of our goals in teaching psychodrama has always been to de-mystify the process by demonstrating to the neophyte director and the uninitiated that there is a beginning, a middle and an end to each session. Each psychodrama is creative and spontaneous and as unique as are individuals. However, there is always a completion, coming "full circle" and achieving closure and healing, to each person in his/her own human drama.

The concepts of insight, integration and change in human behavior are significant phases of any therapeutic process, whether it be individual or group therapy.

Moreno was one of the first exponents of a personality theory stressing the growth-seeking and self-actualizing nature of humans in the context of society. Psychodrama represents a holistic approach which considers the individual in his somatic, psychological and social roles.[12] Moreno's existential system believes in man as his own creator with the power to be spontaneous, ever-changing and self-directing. The group is significant since Moreno saw psychodrama as an extension and intensification of life. Catharsis, insight and integration are possible for the group members as well as the protagonist/client.

Today, psychodrama is applied from many points of view. There seem to be as many varieties of psychodrama and role playing as there are personalities of the directors/therapists. Each one brings to the method his/her own background, ideas, diverse philosophies and creativity.

It is clear now, some seventeen years after meeting and absorbing Moreno, that earlier interests in the work of Adler, Jung and Buber have become integral parts of our philosophical point of view. Along with a strong measure of Moreno, everything we have experienced in life has contributed to our present beliefs which are inherent in our work. Buber says, "man must change his mode of relating himself to each and every being that confronts him. He must affirm other beings as existing in their own right and must not suppress the element of spontaneity that is possible in his relations with them."[13] Alfred Adler's theories, as introduced by Rudolph Dreikurs, state clearly the idea that man's urge to adapt himself to the arbitrary conditions of his environment is expressed by the social interest innate in every human being. "The human community sets three tasks for every individual: Work, which means contributing to the welfare of others; Friendship, which embraces social relationships with comrades and relatives; and Love."[14] Carl Jung believed that all human works have their origins in the inherited powers of creative imagination. All four, Moreno, Buber, Adler and Jung believe in the essential potential of the human being and the human spirit in relationship to his environment, society.

Most human beings go through a large part of their lives saying one thing, thinking another, feeling a third and then proceeding to do a fourth that has nothing to do with the previous three. If one can imagine doing that most of the time, one can begin to see the pulls, the stresses and the fragmentation of the human psyche. One of the many goals of psychodrama is to help the individual integrate his words, thoughts and feelings into his behavior—into his life experience. Another significant goal of psychodrama is to facilitate a wholeness and openness to ourselves and others that we do not learn in our present educational system, where intellectual learning is divorced from life experience. All therapy is really education, the education for life that is not presented to us in schools, nor is it usually taught to us by our primary influences, our parents.

We believe that to fully comprehend what the protagonist is going through in psychodrama, one must have had the experience of being the protagonist. To be a psychodramatist requires human understanding and sensitivity at the deepest level. By totally absorbing all facets of the psychodramatic experience, the practitioner becomes capable of offering the kind of focused, controlled environment that is essential to this treatment modality.

In part, the backgrounds of the authors of this book are action and movement, brought to the psychodramatic method from the theatre and the sport of tennis. Both of these arts require an integration of mind, body and emotions working in unison.

Finally, our personal philosophy regarding each human being's responsibility for self—each one's personal power over his/her actions, decisions and choices, clearly permeates our work.

Martin Buber has said, "Each of us is hiding in a suit of armor, the purpose of which is to protect us from signs. Signs befall us all the time. Life consists in being spoken to, we need only stand still and listen."[15]

Buber tells us to stand still and listen and Moreno teaches us, in addition, to meet the encounter of life and act upon it.

Notes

1. J. L. Moreno, "Reflections on My Methods of Group Psychotherapy," *Ciba Symposium,* II, (1963), p. 148–157.
2. J. L. Moreno, *The Theatre of Spontaneity,* (New York: Beacon House, Inc., 1947).
3. J. L. Moreno, *Sociometry, Experimental Method and the Science of Society,* (New York: Beacon House, Inc., 1951).
4. J. L. Moreno, *Einladung zu Einer Begegnung,* (Vienna: 1914). Trans. J. L. Moreno, *Psychodrama Vol. I,* (New York: Beacon House, Inc., 1977).
5. John Mann, "Evaluation of Group Psychotherapy," *International Handbook of Group Psychotherapy,* Ed. J. L. Moreno, (New York: 1965).
6. Lewis Yablonsky, *Synanon: The Tunnel Back,* (New York: MacMillan, Co., 1967).
7. Hannah B. Weiner, "Treating the Alcoholic with Psychodrama," *Group Psychotherapy,* XVIII, (1965), p. 27–47.
8. Louis A. Fliegler, "Play Acting with the Mentally Retarded," *Exceptional Child,* XVI, (1952), p. 56–60.

9. T. R. Sarbin, "Spontaneity Training of the Feebleminded," *Sociometry,* XVIII, (1952), p. 389–93.

10. Joan Haggerty, Please Can I Play God? (London: 1967).

11. J. L. Moreno, "Reflections on My Methods of Group Psychotherapy," *Ciba Symposium,* II, (1963), p. 148–157.

12. L. J. Fine, "Psychodrama," *Current Psychotherapies,* Ed. Raymond Corsini, Ph.D., (Itasca, Illinois: F. E. Peacock Publishers, 1978), p. 2.

13. Martin Buber, *I and Thou,* (New York: Chas. Scribner's Sons, 1958).

14. Rudolph Dreikurs, *Fundamentals of Adlerian Psychology,* (New York: Greenberg Publishers, 1950).

15. Martin Buber, *I and Thou,* (New York: Chas. Scribner's Sons, 1958).

Section I
Warm-up

Responsibility

We have used the Method of Psychodrama as therapy and taught that method all over the world, one of us since 1967. Since 1974, we have been responsible for the clinical use of psychodrama as a therapy, first in one and then two private psychiatric hospitals. In addition, we have directed the training program in our Institute, supported by the hospitals, where we train professionals in the use of the psychodramatic method. For the past ten years our primary work has centered around the hospitals and training institute. Therefore, we will use our work in these facilities as our model.

The hospital's population includes patients with a variety of diagnoses: situational depression, severe behavior disorders, chemical dependency, schizophrenia, manic depressive illness, psychotic disorders and eating disorders. We see literally everything that might be covered in the Diagnostic and Statistical Manual of Mental Disorders, III. The hospitals are run on a "Programatic System" as follows; General Adult Program, Young Adult Program, Adolescent Program, Older Adult Program, Chemical Dependency Program, Long Term Adolescent Program. Although each of these programs has its own locale and staff within the hospitals, all of the patients from the programs attend psychodrama at the same time. It is our belief that it is essential that all age groups come together at this most significant therapeutic time, since they will, of necessity, come together in life.

Our philosophical base regarding personal responsibility is of such major importance to us that we begin to teach this with our first contact with the patient. Despite the seriousness of the illness, we have certain expectations of each person in the Psychodrama Theatre. When we treat people with the expectation that they will conduct themselves as healthy, attentive individuals, they generally do so. This gives them the self assurance they need to continue attending the sessions and to share their significant feelings and problems in an appropriate manner. If someone is ill and we treat them condescendingly, as if they are too fragile, hostile, obtuse and impotent, we are robbing them of the viable alternatives offered by psychodrama and by life. Often, this is the first opportunity the psychodrama team has to approach the patient and initiate communication. We then attempt to clarify what they have experienced, to relieve them of their anxiety and to dispel the terror of the "unknown." As we enable them to continue attending the sessions, even when fearful, they soon increase their warm-up to becoming protagonist. Prior to a psychodrama session, we often receive reports that a patient is angry, combative and has been disruptive on the unit. Instead of eliminating that patient from the group, we feel that the Psychodrama Theatre is the suitable place for that person. Whatever has to be done can occur safely, psychodramatically and therapeutically in a confidential environment.

The confidentiality of the material disclosed in the session is of utmost importance. Since we have from one to five new patients in the group each day, we reiterate the issue of strict confidentiality before each session begins. The patients are informed that the exceptions are that they may discuss their responses and their identifications to the session with their physicians and nurses. The group does know that a summary is written of each session and placed in the patient's chart. In addition, all significant sharing by group members is charted each day.

We do not read the patient's chart prior to working with that individual as protagonist. We prefer to bring ourselves, as directors, to the session as a *tabula rasa,* clean and without any bias in order to deliver the greatest degree of spontaneity. The only information the nurses present to us concerns physical limitations or extremely unusual circumstances, i.e. patients having psychotic episodes, hallucinations, homicidal ideation, etc.

During the patient sessions, we expect the group members to participate as auxiliary egos. (The auxiliary ego is a person who plays the role of the significant other in the session). "The patient is given the choice of the role and of the assistant with whom he would like to act out the situation. The telic relations of the patient are thus our first guide."[1] According to Moreno, *tele* is the simplest unit of feeling transmitted from one person to another. It is a two-way relationship—a reciprocal non-verbal communication, quite different from empathy, sympathy, transference or counter-transference. Tele is a dual message sending service. I send—you receive, you send—I receive. Tele is the ability to penetrate and understand another person without the necessity of language.

We have developed a system that enables the patient attending their first session to play the role required even though they are unsure of what to do and are often frightened. When the action of the scene begins, one of our team members stands directly behind the patient/auxiliary to be supportive, and when necessary, tells the auxiliary what to say. This enables the patient to stay in the role and often gives the first feeling of accomplishment in months. It also aids in some more direct and powerful channels. For example, we may have a fourteen year-old female who chooses a new, fifty year-old male patient to play the role of her alcoholic father. During the session, we discover that the father is verbally and physically abusive to the child. More often than not, the patient chosen to play father is also alcoholic and abusive to his family. With the help of the team, we enable him to remain in the role and later encourage him to share his own life experience. In revealing his feelings and experiencing the feelings of the young girl, he has given himself the motivation to look into his own behavior and to begin to change his life. The fact that this man was chosen, unknown by the protagonist, is one aspect of Moreno's concept of tele.

When a patient asks or is chosen to be protagonist, our team has certain expectations of that individual. The protagonist must be honest with the director while divulging information about self or others. Although we know that perceptions may be distorted, a basic trust must exist between the director and the subject. To expect less from the patient permits an incongruity in the session.

As directors our expectations are usually unspoken. They reveal themselves during the session through the interaction between director and protagonist. The relationship and interaction between protagonist and director speaks of tele. The method provides the ground rules and the protagonist and director abide by those rules. In doing so, the individual meets a level of achievement he/she did not believe existed.

A prominent component of the tele between the director and the protagonist occurs through the sense of touch. As the director reaches for the protagonist's hand during the move from the group to the stage area, the "tele of touch" has begun. We believe in the importance of touch and we work in close contact, physically, to the protagonist. Touch is the first sense a child learns. His knowledge of love, rejection, anger and need comes through his physical senses. Unfortunately, the instinctive and basic human need for touch has been lost to us through years of acculturation. However, we have yet to find a protagonist who does not respond to touch; to its comfort, to its protection and to its healing effect. Primitive man instinctively knew the therapeutic value of touch. Today, scientists are finally "investigating" the healing power of touch. When working in close proximity to the protagonist, we find the non-verbal cues and body messages are intensified and brought into sharper focus. Conversely, when appropriate and/or necessary, we step back from the individual and the scene for a more objective view.

The director of the psychodrama session must also be responsible for the protagonist, the auxiliaries and the group. The members of the group participate on a feeling level and identify with the material in the session. The group should feel secure in revealing their deepest feelings and in the knowledge that the director will find closure for the session and the group. The director and the team constantly remind the group not to leave the theatre with unresolved feelings or confusion about the session.

Each psychodrama session is dependent upon the spontaneity and creativity of everyone concerned in the session; protagonist, director, auxiliary egos and the group. Moreno has stated that "spontaneity is the arch catalyzer for creativity." Spontaneity is: (1) a new response to an old situation, rather than the same old stereotyped response; (2) an adequate response to a new situation, rather than the inability to deal with something just because it is new; and (3) an adequate response to a combination of the old and new. "Thus the response to a novel situation requires a sense of timing, an imagination for appropriateness. It is a mobility and flexibility of the self, which is indispensable to a rapidly growing organism in a rapidly changing environment."[2] There is also a direct and obvious correlation between spontaneity and anxiety. When our anxiety is up, our spontaneity is down; conversely, when our spontaneity is up, our anxiety is down.

Every *classic, protagonist centered* psychodrama has three essential parts. They are *warm-up, action,* and *sharing.* According to Moreno, no session is complete without these three parts. At appropriate times, there is a fourth part called the *dialogue.* The *warm-up* is the first because we warm up to everything in life, whether we are aware of it or not. The warm-up process serves to prepare the group and the director for the work that is to follow. It fosters group cohesion and trust and enables a protagonist to emerge from the group. The warm-up does not conclude when the action portion begins, but it continues throughout the session as it is necessary to warm the protagonist up to each time and place in the session. The *action* portion is the major segment of the session. This is the movement from scene to scene, using the cues, information and symbols to help the protagonist examine his life and behaviors and to make some choices for the future. The *sharing* is the final closure for the group as well as the protagonist. This takes place when the action portion has concluded for the protagonist. The director, in essence, returns the protagonist to the group. The group is now asked to share something of themselves, of their own lives, their own feelings, as they relate to the experience of the protagonist. The *dialogue* is the time for the director/therapist's feed back and discussion. This can be presented at the conclusion of the sharing or at another time when the protagonist is better able to integrate that information. The dialogue usually depends upon the therapeutic and philosophical orientation of the director. i.e. Freudian, Jungian, Adlerian, etc.

One cannot plan the psychodrama. It is existential and of the moment, born step by step, as the protagonist reveals the necessary information, cues and responses. The director then brings together the "threads" of the session with the aid of the auxiliaries and the group.

The term *protagonist* is taken from the Greek theatre, meaning "first actor" or main character. As protagonist, we are the "stars" of our own psychodramas just as we are the starring characters of our own lives.

"The protagonist is asked to be himself, to portray his own private world . . . he has to act freely, as things rise up in his mind; that is why he has to be given freedom of expression, spontaneity . . . maximum involvement with other subjects and things is not only possible but expected . . . he is stimulated by the use of various psychodramatic techniques to help him to be what he is, more deeply and explicitly than he is in life."[3] *The auxiliary egos* are the arms of the director as they aid in their own way to bring the session to fruition. The auxiliary, playing the role of the significant other, is a moving force in the session. The group involved in the session is not an audience in the inactive sense of being "viewers" of the action, but functions as a microcosm of the world, a miniature society—one where it is safe to play out one's hopes, dreams, fears, realities. "The group has a double purpose. It may serve to help the protagonist or, being itself helped by the subject on the stage it becomes the patient/protagonist . . . it is a sounding board of public opinion . . . it is important to have the presence of a group that is willing to accept and understand him."[4] The creativity and spontaneity of the director is important to the overall movement of the session. "The director has three functions: producer, therapist and analyst . . . as producer, to be on the alert to turn every clue which the subject offers into action, to make the line of the production one with the life line of the subject, and never to let the production lose rapport with the group . . . as therapist attacking and shocking the subject . . . at times indirect and passive. As analyst, he may complement his interpretation by responses coming from informants in the group; husband, wife, parents, children."[5] The director is, indeed, the guide on this inner journey of truth that the protagonist has elected to embark upon in an effort to release his own spontaneity and creativity.

Because of its existential grounding and its reliance on spontaneity, psychodrama is an extremely creative method. No two sessions are alike, as no two human beings are exactly alike. There are numerous psychodramatic techniques, and yet one could witness hundreds of sessions and not see all of the possible techniques available to the psychodramatist. One reason for this is that we use a technique only when it is indigenous to the protagonist at that specific time. Another is that we are constantly creating new techniques or adapting established ones, at the moment, to fit the individual protagonist and session.

There are many techniques that are standard practice for the psychodramatist and a number of "rules" with which to guide the director. The clearest delineation of these rules and standard techniques is in an article written by Zerka T. Moreno, which we will present here with the permission of the author. Although published in 1965, it remains a decisive piece of work to all students of psychodrama.

"Psychodramatic Rules, Techniques and Adjunctive Methods"

Zerka T. Moreno

Rules

"The protagonist acts out his conflicts, instead of talking about them." To this end, a special psychodrama stage may be used, though the process may take place in any informal space available. Ideally, the stage makes for more intense involvement. The process also requires a director, at least one trained auxiliary ego (though the director may act as auxiliary where no one is available). However, maximum learning is achieved wherever such trained assistants are used. Psychodrama may be used as a method of individual treatment, that is, one patient and the director. where it is applied as a method for group treatment, other patients in the group may well serve as auxiliary egos for one another. In this fashion, individually-centered sessions involve other

This article originally appeared in *Group Psychotherapy*, Vol. XXII, 1969. Reprinted by permission of Beacon House Inc.

members of the group, who, in turn, derive therapeutic benefit from this auxiliary ego function.

"The subject acts in the here and now, regardless of when the actual incident took place or may take place, past, present or future, or when the imagined incident was fantasied, or when the crucial situation out of which this present enactment arose, occurred." The subject speaks and acts "in the present", and not in the past, because the past is related to memory and speaking in the past tense removes the subject from the immediacy of the experience, turns him into a spectator or a storyteller rather than an actor. To release spontaneity and increase presentness, the protagonist is specifically instructed to make time his servant, "to act as if this is happening to you now, so that you can feel, perceive and act as if this were happening to you for the first time." "The subject must act out "his truth", as he feels and perceives it, in a completely subjective manner (no matter how distorted this appears to the spectator)." The process cannot proceed properly unless we accept the patient with all his subjectivity. Enactment comes first, re-training comes later. We must give him the satisfaction of act completion first, before re-training for behavior changes.

"The patient is encouraged to maximize all expression, action, and verbal communication, rather than reduce it." To this end, delusions, hallucinations, soliloquies, thoughts, fantasies, projections, are all allowed to be part of the production. Again, restraint has to come after expression, though it should never be overlooked.

"The warming-up process proceeds from the periphery to the center." The director will, therefore, not begin with the most traumatic events in the patient's life. The commencement is on a more superficial level, allowing the self-involvement of the patient to carry him more deeply towards the core. The director's skills will be expressed in the construction of the scenes and the choice of persons or objects needed to assist the patient in his warming up.

"Whenever possible, the protagonist will pick the time, the place, the scene, the auxiliary ego he requires in the production of his psychodrama". The director and protagonist are partners; at one moment the director may be more active, but the protagonist reserves the right to decline the enactment of or the changing of a scene.

"Psychodrama is just as much a method of restraint as it is a method of expression." The repressiveness of our culture has attached to "expression per se" a value which is often beyond its actual reward. In such methods as role reversal, or enactment of roles which require re-

*REPRESSIVNESS OF OUR CULTURE

9

straint and/or reconditioning of excitability, lies a greatly underestimated application of psychodrama. For example, the chronic bad actor in life, the delinquent or psychopath, whose ability for self-restraint has not been strengthened by his warming up to stresses in life.

"The patient is permitted to be as unspontaneous or inexpressive as he is at this time." This may seem to be a contradiction to the rule on spontaneity, but is not. Thus "maximizing of expression" may also refer to the patient's inability to express his withdrawal, his submerged anger. Gradually the director will try to release the patient from his own bonds by various psychodramatic methods. The fact that a patient lacks in spontaneity is not a block to psychodramatic production. This is the reason for the existence of the auxiliary egos who are trained to support the patient. The person who is unable to be spontaneous as himself, in his own roles, may become extremely spontaneous in role reversal with others. His expressiveness will grow as his spontaneity increases.

"The protagonist must learn to take the role of all of those with whom he is meaningfully related, to experience those persons in his social atom, their relationship to him and to one another." The patient must learn to "become" in psychodrama that which he sees, feels, hears, smells, dreams, loves, hates, fears, rejects, is rejected by, wants to avoid, wants to become. The patient has "taken unto himself" with greater or lesser success, those persons, situations, experiences and perceptions from which he is now suffering. In order to overcome the distortions and manifestations of imbalance, he has to reintegrate them on a new level. Role reversal is one of the methods of achieving this, so that he can grow beyond those experiences which are of negative impact, free himself and become more spontaneous along positive lines.

"The director must trust the psychodrama method as the final arbiter and guide in the therapeutic process." When the warm-up of the director is objective and there is no anxiety in his performance, then the psychodramatic method becomes flexible, an all embracing medium leading systematically to the heart of the patient's problem, enabling the director, the protagonist, the auxiliary egos and the group members to become a cohesive force, welded into maximal emotional learning.

"Psychodrama sessions consist of three portions: The warm-up, the action portion and the post-action sharing by the group." Disturbances in any one of these areas reflect upon the total process. However, "sharing" may at times be of a non-verbal nature instead of verbal. In any event, the director must see that all three portions evolve from every session.

"Warming up to psychodrama may proceed differently from culture to culture and appropriate changes in the application of the method should be made." What may be a suitable warm-up in Manhattan may fall flat elsewhere. Cultural and regional adaptations must be made by the director.

"The protagonist should never be left with the impression that he is alone with this type of problem in this group." The director must draw from the group, in the post-action discussion phase, identifications with his subject. This will establish mutually satisfying relations among group members, increase cohesion and broaden interpersonal perceptions. It is not analysis that is indicated in this phase, but love and sharing of the self. The only way to repay a person for giving of himself is in kind. This will frequently warm up others in the audience to come forward in a similar manner and helps to establish closure.

Techniques

Psychodrama begins with the warm-up, verbal or physical, which changes from culture to culture, and is dependent upon the individual director and his relationship to the group and the protagonist (client, patient, subject). However, the warm-up must lead to a concrete situation in which the protagonist finds himself face to face with his fellow man. With neither practice nor preparation the patient now plays the part of himself in the particular situation. The patient's father, mother, wife, friend, foe and employer are not present in the flesh, but are played by so-called auxiliary egos, i.e., trained assistants or fellow group members. Psychodramatic confrontation is a potent method of dispelling forms of behavior which in life are threatening, painful or troublesome. With the aid of "surplus reality" techniques, it is possible to confront and examine those incompletely experienced or unexpressed nuances of reality in a manner which may be impossible to do in actual situations.

One of the most effective of these techniques is role reversal. The protagonist is compelled through role reversal to feel his way into a particular person who is significant in his life. Since he must take the role of that person within the psychodramatic setting, and in relationship to himself, he begins to get a deeper understanding of that person. Thus the protagonist has the opportunity to experience his environment, himself, and others from a different vantage point than the one to which he is accustomed. By doing so, he is both breaking through the remnants of childhood egocentricity and sharpening his social sensitivity.

When using the <u>Double method</u>, an auxiliary ego imitates the bearing and physical movement of the protagonist. As soon as the protagonist falls into inner conflict, the auxiliary speaks the thoughts, feelings and impulses which are not really apprehended by him. In this way, psychodrama brings about a type of catharsis of experience. This method is an excellent starting point in reaching the highly introverted, socially isolated protagonist. <u>Multiple</u> doubles may be used to represent and embody the various aspects of the protagonist's psyche. These may be represented by his desires, conflicts, assets, shortcomings or the varying roles he plays in life as father, husband, employee or any other role. This technique is used to help him to free him from the crippling restraints of self-rejection and hyper-self-criticism.

The <u>soliloquy technique</u> is another useful tool in opening the psyche to a more subtle range of experience. The director may stop the action at one point and ask the protagonist to turn aside and speak his feelings at that moment in the action.

The <u>mirror technique</u> enables the protagonist to see himself as others see him. While he watches from the audience, members of the group "mirror" his behavior on the psychodrama stage. This may help to clarify any discrepancies between his self-perception and what he communicates of himself to others. Thus the mirror technique helps to sensitize the protagonist to the reality of how other people experience him.

In the <u>future projection</u> the patient portrays in action how he thinks his future will shape itself. He picks the point in time, the place and the people whom he expects to be involved with at that time. By thus concretizing a conceivable future event it is possible for the protagonist to get some feeling of the actual future situation.

There are other techniques such as <u>dream presentation</u>, <u>retraining of the dream</u>, <u>family therapy</u>, <u>psychodramatic shock</u>, <u>personality assessment</u>, and many others. And within the framework of the general techniques described above, many trained and creative directors use other methods to bring to completion the action portion of the psychodrama.

The final portion of the psychodrama is the sharing. Here the group or audience is encouraged to relate to the protagonist in a non-analytical and non-judgmental manner. They are asked to identify with him, to relate those aspects of their own experience which are similar to or have a bearing upon the experiences of the protagonist as brought out in the process of the psychodrama. This process of sharing thus helps to link the protagonist with his environment rather than alienating him from it.[6]

The standard techniques, as well as new and unusual ones will be discussed where appropriate and in conjunction with their use within specific sessions.

The Four Primary Techniques

The work of the psychodramatist requires varied skills and knowledge, not only in the form of action, but also in the use of interpretation, analysis and hypotheses. The director should not attempt the aforementioned too early in the session. To make a hypothesis or an assumption based on some early information may well lead the director down the wrong path. It is important to gather all of the information, actionally, as one moves through the session. The director must file the significant cues, watching for patterns and/or repeated actions, messages and situations. These cues should be used psychodramatically when appropriate for the protagonist. In this sense, the autonomy of the individual is always present and honored. We must enable the individual to explore wherever necessary, but we should essentially remain the guide.

The first techniques to be learned and understood by the director are: *warm-up; scene setting;* the use of the *auxiliary ego as significant other and as double;* and the concept and use of *role reversal.* As we continue our discussion of the psychodramatic method, you will note a number of terms and techniques that are used and not defined. There is a glossary in this book that lists and defines these terms and techniques.

Warm-up is first and is basic in psychodrama because it is an intrinsic part of life. Moreno stated that we warm up to everything in life, whether we are aware of it or not. We warm up to rising, going to bed, eating and preparing for work. It may be a negative warm-up, but nevertheless, it is a warm-up. At the simplest level, the way in which we warm up to anything in life is the way we "prepare" for that event, and that preparation/warm-up is the stepping stone to the consequences of that event. It is important that the director find ways to warm up to the role of director as well as warming up the group and the protagonist.

In psychodrama, warm-up takes many forms and there are many types of warm-ups. There are structured warm-ups, informal warm-ups, group warm-ups and warm-ups designed to produce a protagonist. In our setting we usually have a long list of individuals waiting to become protagonist. Nevertheless, it is important to have a daily warm-up when the group has been separated for any length of time. The purpose is to warm everyone up to each other and to the director; the director to the group; and everyone to the work at hand.

The daily warm-up quickly sets the climate and the tone of the session. When the group has been separated, even for a day, people have had a variety of experiences in the interim. They have been drawn away and need to re-establish themselves within the framework of a psychodrama group. Since we are in an in-patient setting, we have daily changes as new people enter the hospital and others are discharged. Each addition or subtraction of an individual changes the structure and the sociometry of the group.

We use a number of simple, yet provocative, warm-ups that integrate the new members as well as produce information regarding the whole group. The first task is to help the group to be in touch with themselves and their own feelings. We begin by asking them to close their eyes for a moment and to be aware of their bodies and their breathing. We then ask them to focus on one of a number of specific themes. This could be any of the following suggestions or one that is appropriate for your group. For example: What is the strongest feeling you are having at this moment? What person or event makes you angry? What one behavior of yours would you like to change? What person in your life has had some influence on you, positive or negative? What day in your life do you consider most significant?

As the director moves around the group from one individual to another, we ask for that person's name and the answer to the original question. The name, obviously, helps us to remember whatever that particular individual has shared with us in that opening warm-up. We may ask an additional question or two depending upon the answer we receive. Our aim, here, is to get specific answers. When we get a general answer, we must probe further. When we have completed the warm-up round, we ask someone in the group to name everyone. This has become an enjoyable ritual as the patients vie with each other to name everyone in the room. Since our groups are very large, it is an achievement for a patient to name thirty people. This is particularly true when the patient has recently entered the hospital in a deep depression.

In life, and in the psychodrama session, the warm-up does not stop at the outset of the session but continues when the next phase begins and is produced anew throughout the session. The purpose of the structured warm-ups is for a protagonist to emerge from the group—ready and warmed-up to work.

Once the protagonist emerges and the *presenting problem* has been established, the next step is *scene setting.* Finding a recent scene that is representative of the protagonist's problem and then anchoring ourselves in time, space and reality are important for the protagonist, the director, the auxiliaries and the group. The protagonist places the simple chairs and pads and produces the space where he/she feels: "depressed," "lost," "angry," "cold," etc. We are all listening, watching and picking up cues about the protagonist and the environment with which the individual surrounds self. At the same time, the protagonist is warming up to that time and place so that we can enact the scene in the existential here and now; Moreno's "hic et nunc." The steps in scene setting are clear and logical and when done in order, help the director to keep people, places and events clearly in mind for later use. First are the elements of the location: when?, where? and which room? The protagonist should physically place the objects in space. We now need the *significant object,* who lives here, or doesn't live here, and who is explicitly in the scene. If a thirteen year old protagonist tells us that mother and he live in this house, we must ask, "Where is father?" Obviously, it can make a tremendous difference to the total session if we know whether father is dead, has divorced mother, lives elsewhere or is merely away on business. Second, comes the choosing of auxiliary egos, by the protagonist, to enact the roles of others in the scene. At this stage, we often have the protagonist choose the significant others who are *not* in this scene. Our object in obtaining the significant other(s) at this time is to retain the warm-up for the protagonist since we know they will be needed later. Often the "missing people" are as significant, or more significant, than those present. i.e. the father who doesn't live here, the child who has run away or the spouse who is dead. Third, are the descriptions or presentations of the auxiliaries who will enact the roles. With these three steps, we are continually collecting data for the oncoming scene and for the entire session.

The use of the *auxiliary ego* is essential to the movement of the session. The auxiliary as other can: increase the protagonist's warm up to time and place and reality; intensify the action; help gather information; and in the reverse role, can exaggerate and mirror the protagonist. The auxiliary can represent values, virtues and morals as well as being the significant other. When appropriate, the auxiliary can be God, the Devil, good, evil, etc.

The auxiliary, as double, is a powerful agent for the protagonist and director. There are many types of doubles and any number of uses for this technique. One may use multiple doubles for different times and/or ages of the protagonist. Opposing doubles may be used to help intensify polarities within the protagonist. Any number of doubles may be used to delineate the many facets, roles, and/or parts of the protagonist. The auxiliary, as double, places his/her body in the position of the protagonist, not to imitate, but to feel what the protagonist is feeling. On a deeper level, the double is there to assist and explore the innermost feelings of the protagonist. These are often feelings the protagonist is too fearful to articulate or feelings the individual has not allowed to surface. Working with patients has taught us to use the double in new and creative ways. Our trained doubles verbalize prudently, proceeding from the *periphery to the core,* which allows the acceptance of the double. In moving slowly and cautiously, the information is more likely to come from the protagonist than the double. This is more productive since it is the protagonist's own words that are most important. With this in mind, the double uses techniques such as sentence completion, a hint of the feeling rather than labeling, or paradoxical intent, all for the purpose of allowing the protagonist to define his/her own feeling.

When using a double, it is essential that the director check with the protagonist for the accuracy of the doubling. This is another method of retaining the autonomy of the protagonist as opposed to implanting the bias of the double or the director. The double should certainly explore, try a number of options and use spontaneity, but it is the responsibility of the director to keep the session from being contaminated by auxiliaries. There are several simple, clear ways to check the doubling. The director can ask the protagonist, "is that correct?," "is that close?," and/or "put that in your own words." This is particularly important when working with patients who are often so anxious to please that we must be certain we are dealing with the protagonist's actual feelings. The double is often in the best position for exploration. Issues that may be intrusive from the director evolve naturally and easily from the double. The double can: explore the protagonist's psyche without showing bias; negotiate options as the ally; dispel hostility and/or resistance toward the director; and convey the truth when the protagonist is having difficulty owning that reality.

We have worked with patients who have needed more than the traditional double. One patient had removed herself from reality and become secluded in her own terror filled world. She cowered in the fetal position seemingly unaware of our presence. The double assumed the identical physical position and moved closer and closer to the protagonist with caution until she was huddled beside her, bodies touching. Moments later, the double began to moan, quietly at first, then at the same pitch as the protagonist. During this period the only recognition of the double by the protagonist was the infinitesimal movement of her body. The physical closeness, the warmth of the bodies touching, the verbal sounds of communion enabled the double to enter the protagonist's world. The double, sensing the protagonist's need to be close, allowed her creativity to emerge. With the boundaries removed, the double crawled inside the patient's cocoon. The protagonist began to trust the double as her only ally. The double slowly began to exaggerate the sounds and movements of the patient, expanding on the negative life threatening soliloquy. As the double became more vigorous, the protagonist's affect changed. She was listening and seeing a mirror of herself. The double, aware of the change, began to alter her soliloquy to a more positive one and a slow transformation took place in the protagonist. A form of role reversal was occurring as the protagonist integrated the strength of the double. The double then became less dominant and the protagonist was enabled to emerge from her cocoon which had kept her withdrawn from life. Within a week, we were able to work with the patient in a full, reality based session.

Role reversal, a major technique, is the procedure of the protagonist becoming the significant other. The role reversal should be used at strategic times within the session. It is important that the director understand the concept and use of role reversal to aid the protagonist and auxiliary in completing that function.

When asking a protagonist to reverse roles, it is necessary to warm that individual up to the role of the other. The wife, role reversing with an auxiliary playing the role of husband is asked to assume the physical posture of husband, to feel as husband is feeling at that time and to speak only as husband in that role. In a role reversal, the auxiliary should physically change places with the protagonist and repeat the last lines the protagonist has spoken. This is necessary because the protagonist must hear his/her words while in the role of the other. This also aids the protagonist in warming up to the role of the other.

Role reversal is used for specific purposes: (1) At the simplest level, role reversal is necessary to obtain information that is only known by the protagonist. This role reversal gives the auxiliary the information and the manner of presentation of the "other." (2) Role reversal is used when it is necessary for the protagonist to understand and feel the sensibility of the other. This role reversal can bring about greater telic sensitivity between people. (3) Role reversal is used to help the protagonist see self through the "eyes of the other," a form of mirror which produces insight for the protagonist. (4) Role reversal is used to aid the spontaneity of the protagonist and to remove his/her defenses. An adolescent in his own role, will complain only about the parent's "strict rules." In role reversal, as the parent, he will begin to list all of his actual negative behaviors. (5) Role reversal is used when the protagonist is the only one to answer the question or to give advice about self. For example, the protagonist is in a surplus reality scene with a revered, dead parent, and asks advice concerning a serious decision. The director must role reverse the protagonist into the other for that answer. Although the auxiliary, in the role of the parent, may be warmed up to that role, he/she should not be allowed to give that answer or advice. It is the responsibility of the protagonist to make his/her own decisions and choices, while in the role of the other in the scene.

Notes

1. J. L. Moreno, *Psychodrama Vol. I,* (New York: Beacon House, Inc., 1964), p. 183.
2. Ibid.
3. J. L. Moreno, Monograph from a speech in Chicago, (1946).
4. Ibid.
5. Ibid.
6. Zerka T. Moreno, "Psychodramatic Rules, Techniques and Adjunctive Methods," *Group Psychotherapy,* XVIII, (1965), p. 73–86.

Section II

Action

Content and Process

The action begins for the patient with the individual's first group warm-up. We quickly differentiate between the content and process of the patient's responses and begin to assess that patient as a potential protagonist.

The difference between content and process is a fundamental concept indigenous to all therapies, but one we find many psychodramatists fail to recognize. It is all too easy, particularly in psychodrama, to become caught up in the "story" and to play out scenes only involved in content. *Content* is the subject matter. It is the individual's story. *Process* is the manner in which the individual responds internally to the content and how he/she then acts in life. "Psychodrama by its nature should attend specifically to process. Enactment makes process events vivid and explicit as they occur."[1]

A protagonist may become extremely angry in the first scene. This could be the content, not the process, and if we do not differentiate this, we might play out the entire session revolving only around anger. Rather than immediately allow a catharsis of anger, we need to see several scenes or fragments and find the *essence* of each. What we discover is that the protagonist easily gets angry in all situations. What he is really feeling is inadequacy, and he covers this feeling with anger. In this case, the anger is content—the story. The process of this protagonist reveals that when he is feeling inadequate, he gets angry. Once we have clarified the difference for the protagonist and ourselves, we can move on to the earlier times in his life when he has felt inadequate and help him to find the threads that have produced that feeling. It is only then that we can help him to change his process.

To aid the director/therapist in distinguishing clearly between process and content, we have developed a series of focusing techniques. These techniques were developed through our work with hospitalized patients, who were in need of clear, precise questions and directions.

Focusing Techniques

Focusing consists of a number of broad concepts as well as some distinct ideas. First, we make every attempt to enable the individual to answer all questions specifically rather than generally. This means that questions must be geared toward specific answers. i.e. A patient responding to a question regarding her anger will say, "Everyone makes me angry." When asked, "Who in your own life makes you angry?,"

21

the response may be, "My whole family." Instead of accepting this, we ask a more narrowing question. "Which member of your family makes you the most angry?" The answer usually comes immediately and spontaneously, "My husband," or "My mother," or the significant other in each case. Obviously, stating the specific person or issue is more productive for both the individual and the director than statements like, "I'm depressed about everything," or "I hate everyone."

A second concept of focusing is the limiting of descriptions. We discovered early in our work with patients that it was literally impossible to use the traditional method of presenting the characters in the scene. It was much too confusing to have them role reverse into the auxiliaries in the scene in order to achieve the information needed about the other. We also discovered that these early and numerous role reversals by the protagonist caused the loss of warm-up to the scene.

Therefore, when introducing characters, we limit the descriptions and obtain precise information about the other as perceived by the protagonist. We ask questions like, "What two words would you use to describe your father's personality?" The answer comes quickly and directly, "domineering and cold." We ask for "a word or symbol to describe the relationship with father?," the answer, "master and slave." We have discovered that this system enables the protagonist to be spontaneous and creative, to think and speak and act in symbols and metaphors rather than to tell us long stories about what has happened.

Another focusing technique is to extract the *main message* from the significant others in the scene. Again, rather than enact a long scene in order to extract the essence, we focus on the actions and feelings by getting the main message of the significant others. We can then extract the primary feeling of the protagonist. This also aids in an *intensification* of feelings as we often have the messages repeated. All of this helps to avoid the lengthy content and allows us to focus on the process of the protagonist, which gives the insight into self that is needed to change behavior.

In helping the protagonist to warm up to a specific age, time and place, we use provocative focusing techniques. Simple questions that require specific answers warm up the individual and also give the director and auxiliaries much needed information. For example, "You are eight years old—what do you like most in your life?" Then, "What do you hate the most?" The answers, again, are spontaneous and informative. "I like to hide in my tree house" and "I hate going home, they are always fighting."

When the protagonist is unable to separate emotions or to clearly identify what is being felt, we find ways to help him/her focus on one emotion at a time. i.e. The protagonist professes anger, but whenever faced with the circumstances of that emotion, is only able to cry. We ask to hold the tears for a few moments. We hold out our hands for the tears and, in pantomime, put them aside. The protagonist is then able to be in touch with the appropriate feeling. Needless to say, in doing this, as in any surplus reality, one must enable the protagonist into the "willing suspension of disbelief." (See glossary)

Included in the total focusing process is a concentration on the body. We believe in the wholeness of the human being and that one cannot separate body, mind and emotions. The body gives us messages constantly and we must attend to those messages. A supplementary advantage in focusing on the body is an opportunity to deal with psychosomatic illness. In particular, we deal with the common ones of stomach pains, migraine headaches, back aches and respiratory problems. Our use of the body is intended to help the protagonist be in touch with primary feelings and to intensify those feelings when appropriate to the session and the protagonist. When a protagonist is unable to verbalize a feeling, asking him/her to "put their body in the shape of the feeling" or asking, "Where in your body do you feel it the most?," generates the feeling and subsequently the verbalization and the understanding needed. In thousands of sessions, with every possible kind of protagonist, we have yet to find an individual who cannot locate the feeling in his/her body. It is important to state here that we do not use "body language interpretation" in the general sense that has become common. We do not feel that a certain body posture has a particular meaning. Our stress on the body is individual to that protagonist at that time. Often two people with the same emotion show that emotion differently with their bodies. However we are always aware of body cues that may be symbolically significant later in the session. i.e. the fetal position.

Symbols and Signs

A significant part of our work is in the constant attention to symbols, covertly or overtly given by the protagonist. Man is inherently a symbol maker. We human beings speak and think in symbols and metaphors more than we are cognizant of in our daily lives. ". . . the human brain is constantly carrying on a process of symbolic transformation

. . . as a basic human need."[2] Many of us in our modern society have lost our spontaneity. "We have lost our life-symbols, and our actions no longer have ritual value; this is the most disastrous hindrance to the free functioning of the human mind."[3] Therefore, we feel that making the protagonist aware of his symbols helps to retrieve that lost spontaneity, the "free functioning" of the mind that is vital to life.

We have taught ourselves and teach our students to hear the symbols and carefully note them. Every therapist needs *selective hearing* in order to pick up the important cues. Whether one uses them immediately or later, to concretize or to give insight, they are ever present and significant. We constantly hear simple phrases like, "I feel trapped," "I'm in a black hole," "I'm carrying a heavy load." When symbols are repeated, even though the exact words are not echoed, the psychodramatist must listen since they are vital to the protagonist and to the total session.

During the training at Beacon under the tutelage of Zerka Moreno, the students were taught to always ask for a *significant object* when setting the scene. We have become increasingly aware of how many psychodramatists do not ask that, and thereby miss important cues and information. We feel that the objects people surround themselves with are not only significant but can be used symbolically within the session. This creatively places the protagonist in touch with the past, a significant other, a long forgotten strength, or his/her own potential.

A timid, frightened individual who indicated a stuffed toy lion as a significant object early in her session was role reversed into the "lion" at the appropriate time, which enabled her suppressed courage to surface. "To understand what people are and what they might become, it helps to understand what things they cherish and why."[4]

A study was made in 1974 on the relationship between people and objects. The social scientists, Czikszentimihalyi and Rochberg-Halton, have turned their findings into a book, The Meaning of Things: Domestic Symbols and the Self. They discovered that people rarely cherish their possessions for aesthetic reasons, but "because they help them relive memorable occasions and pleasing relationships. They cherished things . . . for the information they conveyed about the owner and his or her ties to others."[5] We have been involved in many sessions where the significant object becomes the key to the entire session. "It is intriguing to consider the psychological value . . . of easily broken objects. . . . A china cup preserved over a generation is a victory of human purpose over chaos, an accomplishment to be quietly cherished."[6]

Fantasies, Dreams and Hallucinations

When one learns to think symbolically and actionally (psychodramatically) in tandem, then it becomes a natural method to use with dreams, hallucinations, fantasies and unconscious material. The psychodramatist enters the dream, fantasy or hallucinatory material and *sees what the protagonist sees.* In this way, we can help the individual deal with this material and make sense of what seems to be "senseless."

For clarity in the evolvement of fantasy, the director should make the transition from *fantasy to symbolism to reality.* There are many fantasy techniques for use in warm-ups and within the session. All are viable and useful techniques. However, if they remain in the realm of fantasy and do not move to reality, they lose their therapeutic potency for the protagonist. The Magic Shop and the Mask Shop are fantasy techniques usually employed as warm-ups to secure a protagonist. We begin the Magic Shop fantasy with a question. "What value or virtue would you most like to purchase?" We progress to the symbolism of what that request represents to that individual. Finally, once we find a protagonist and begin the session, we anchor ourselves in time, space and reality. Similarly, a director may turn the protagonist into a fantasized childhood hero during the session. However, we must then be able to relate the symbolism of that "hero" to the protagonist, and finally, to whatever similar qualities the protagonist possesses in reality for use in his present life.

Hallucinatory material can move in that same pattern. In the material that is brought to the surface are the individual's personal symbols. These can be brought into his/her individual reality. For example, we dealt with a young college girl who had been brought to the hospital after a suicidal and homicidal episode. She was hallucinating a horrible green devil who was in control of her. We entered into the hallucination, seeing the devil along with her. We used an auxiliary, the lights and sound to produce her "devil." At the appropriate time, we helped her to move from the fantasized green devil to the symbol of being controlled. Finally, when she had the act gratification of the director and team seeing what she saw, we asked a reality based question. When we asked who the devil really was, we discovered *he* was father who had sexually molested the girl since childhood. As we arrived at reality, she no longer needed the hallucination.

One use of dream presentation is to re-train the dream or the recurring nightmare. In this instance, the individual enacts the nightmare as it is dreamed and then re-enacts it in a new and more positive way. We have had success in re-training recurring nightmares of Viet Nam veterans who previously were unable to divest themselves of the horrors of their wartime experiences.

Dream presentations also fit into the concept of transition from the dream, to the symbolism, to the reality. One may begin a session with a dream presentation. As the symbols within the dream become apparent to the protagonist and director, the dream then moves into a psychodrama session. Since dreams are often representative of our unconscious thoughts, they give us excellent material to carry into the conscious work of the psychodrama.

The Psychodramatic Spiral

We think symbolically and actionally, therefore we see the psychodramatic process as an active symbol. To this end we have devised a visual teaching aid that enables the student and/or psychodramatist to track each session from presenting problem through the concluding, sharing phase of the session. This is the *Psychodramatic Spiral* which consists of three concentric circles, each one smaller than the preceding one. This has the effect of a spiral when looking down at it from above. (Figure A Page 27) After this spiral was developed, we realized that it is also the figure of Moreno's psychodrama stage in reverse. Moreno's stage builds upward, like a three tiered wedding cake, each level smaller than the preceding one. Moreno considered the first level the warm-up level, with each succeeding movement going toward the top level of the stage. The psychodramatic concepts as stated by Zerka T. Moreno are that we should move *from the periphery to the core* and that the session should come *full circle,* back to the present. These concepts are clarified by our vision of the psychodramatic process as a spiral. As we move from the outer edges of the protagonist's problem, the story, to the core underneath, we are dealing with process rather than content. From the outer surface or armor of the individual, we are progressing to his/her inner core of sensibility. The spiral becomes the *map* of the session.

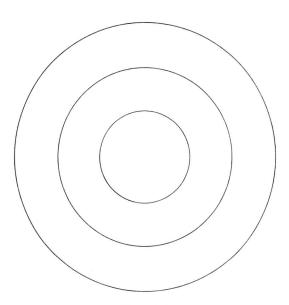

Figure A

We must begin with the *presenting problem*. The presenting problem can be a situation, a feeling, a problem, a relationship, or whatever the individual needs to examine in his/her life. Then we ask for a scene, a recent time and place that demonstrates the presenting problem or difficulty. It is important to begin in the present whenever possible. We live in the present and therefore must know and understand the protagonist's present life situations. Only then can we make the necessary connections to the protagonist's process in life, past and present.

All sessions will not move in the exact order described. It may be necessary to move backward and forward in time. There will be occasions when it is not possible to begin in the present because the protagonist is too resistive or too warmed up to a past scene. When that occurs, one follows the protagonist to the scene in the past and allows the enactment, culling the information. As soon as feasible, we must go to the present to discover the current life situations and processes of the protagonist. We have experienced directors who go immediately to the past and/or to a scene that seems very dramatic before exploring the protagonist's present. For example, we saw a director encourage the protagonist's anger at husband for withholding love and conclude with a reconciliation scene with husband. In reality, if the director had begun in the present, he would have discovered that the protagonist was a child abuser and an alcoholic. There was no possible reconciliation with husband, who had already filed for divorce. What was needed for this protagonist was to understand her actions in the present, see what the connections in the past might be and assume responsibility for the changes necessary in her life.

We will use the following model to describe and explain the movement of the psychodramatic process. We have included in this book a section of actual sessions, directed with patients, and we have tracked these sessions on the spiral. As we describe this prototype of the process, you will note a number of terms and techniques that are used and not explained. There is a glossary that lists and defines those terms and techniques.

A Prototype Session

For our purposes here we will use the term *scene* to mean the time and place we are reproducing in the session. However, scene can mean an actual scene, an action sociogram, a fragment of time and space or any specific segment of the session.

We begin with the presenting problem. (See Figure B Page 29). If the protagonist takes us to a scene at the office (scene 1), we will allow that enactment and extract its essence. However, that is usually not enough information in the present, and we need to see a social situation or a scene at home. (scene 2) Then we begin the journey back into the recent past. i.e. If the scene at home (scene 2) reveals that the protagonist is living with mate number two, we must see a scene that typifies the first marriage and/or the divorce. (scene 3)

We begin to see some patterns, some repeated cues, descriptions and messages as we move back in time. Often the difficulties at work (scene 1) and at home (scene 2) are similar to those in the first marriage. (scene 3) They may be different in content, but the process in each case is similar. First mate may have been loud and abusive and the second mate may be quiet and withdrawn. Although they are different, the process by which they interact with the protagonist may well be the same. i.e. "Master and Slave" or "Father and Child."

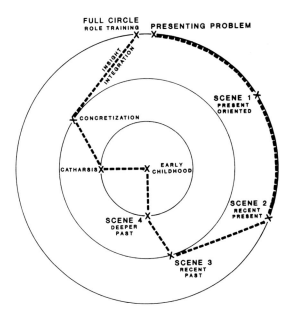

Figure B

The protagonist may now take us to a scene at an earlier age when the feelings and the essence of the previous scenes are similar. (scene 4) Throughout we are listening, watching and picking up cues in order to be in touch with the significant feelings and behaviors of the protagonist. The information, the cues, the overt symbols are all filed by the director for future use in the session.

We have been moving from the periphery to the core, deeper and deeper, not only back in time but deeper into the psyche of the protagonist. What is most important to remember throughout this process is the on-going warm-up, the continuing preparation for each scene, sociogram or fragment. For example, if we do not prepare the protagonist, we will have a contrived, "half-remembered" thirty-two year old perception of what happened at five years old instead of a deeply present and felt re-enactment of an old experience.

It is also important to keep in mind that the protagonist is the star of the session, not the auxiliary egos nor the director no matter how dramatic those other roles seem to be.

The protagonist will take us, finally, to an early childhood scene. Here we find the origins of the primary feelings and the presenting problem. (By presenting problem we mean not only the original presenting problem, but what may have surfaced as the real problem. Often the original presenting problem is a screen for what is really troubling the protagonist.)

Next, when appropriate, we help the protagonist experience a *catharsis* (of anger, tears, primal scream) which then starts us on our outward journey from the core. As we reach this climax of the session, we, as directors, must remember the importance of clarity. The protagonist must understand the motivations and actions of self as well as those of the significant others. i.e. If the repressed anger began in childhood, the protagonist must be helped to differentiate the old anger at mother from the present anger at self for maintaining the patterns developed in the past. Too often, individuals rationalize present destructive and negative behavior by blaming past events and/or people. Confronting self instead of blaming others is often the most difficult part of the session for the individual. When one has the willingness to look at self, at how he/she has contributed to what has happened to them, he/she is also prepared to confront his/her conscious and unconscious.

The next step is what we call the *concretization*. This segment is where all of the threads of the session, all of the pieces of the puzzle come together. On many levels we have been making issues and feelings "concrete" throughout the session by putting them into action using any number of psychodramatic techniques. (Body work, focusing, surplus reality, mirror.) This final concretization is developed from the protagonist's own symbols. The protagonist is using symbols and metaphors throughout the session that apply directly and concretely to his/her situation and life. These symbols are the ones that are called into use for concretization.

This stage is where our personal philosophy and bias is most evident. It is our belief that every human being can be responsible for his/her choices in life. They can choose to bring growth and productivity into their lives, or they can continue to do whatever it is that makes them feel depressed, useless, impotent and manipulated. Therefore, it is important at this stage to make use of the protagonist's most significant and evident symbols. As the concretization is being structured, we clarify the symbols we have been given. The protagonist must understand that he/she may not have had control of their life at age five, but now at thirty-two must make the choice and live out the consequences of that choice.

An example of a concretization could be the use of a symbol noted earlier. "I feel trapped." We have the protagonist describe the "trap" visually and then have the individual build that trap with the simple chairs and equipment we have available. Remember it is the individual's symbol and his/her descriptions of that symbol that are necessary. When the trap has been built, we ask the protagonist to delineate the parts of self that make up the trap. i.e. fear of failure, fear of rejection. The protagonist must then deal with those facets of self that keep him/her in the trap.

The concretization is an important step in the movement toward closure. We began in the present and opened the "Pandora's Box" of the protagonist's psyche. We saw, in action, the protagonist's process. Therefore, we must come to an ending, a closure, for the protagonist and for the group. In addition to clarifying the protagonist's responsibility for change, the concretization should be used to validate his/her strengths and options in life. The concretization, whenever possible, should conclude on a *high* note or some positive possibility. Human beings move and change at their own pace. Generally, it is wiser to avoid a concretization that the director feels might not end on a positive note. The director should be able to gauge the protagonist's ego strength, weaknesses and potential for action—in the session and in life.

There may be times when the protagonist's choice is to remain with the status quo no matter how depressing, painful or difficult. To change seems too risky, or the pay-off for being sick too tempting. In such a case, rather than present this conclusion as a failure, we must make clear to the patient that he/she is not ready to change at this time, and we can accept that choice.

The concretization should be present oriented even if some elements of past actions and feelings are included. We are now coming out through the spiral and through the individual's life, back to the present. As we have moved from the core of our spiral with the climax and the concretization, both *insight* and *integration* have begun. Throughout, it is essential that the protagonist be aware of feelings, thoughts and actions. The link between the *affective* and the *cognitive* is necessary for the protagonist to integrate the session, even though he/she may not be able to completely integrate everything at the close of the session.

Along the journey we might have shown the protagonist any number of things through a variety of psychodramatic techniques. We could have used a mirror to show the individual his behavior in action or to see how he/she is reflecting mother or father's behavior. We could have seen several action sociograms to demonstrate behaviors in different situations, times or families.

We have come almost full circle at this point, back to the present and to the responsibility of the protagonist. Whenever possible we come full circle, to the original problem we have been tracking. This is best done by returning to the first scene or the first indication of the primary problem(s), and re-enacting that scene with the protagonist using the new insights and responsibilities. This becomes an excellent *role training scene*. Another option might be a *future projection* where the protagonist uses his/her new found spontaneity and creativity.

In the preceding discussion and diagram we have used eight scenes or segments. This does not mean that every session will consist of eight or more segments; many will have less. There is no specific number of scenes for any given session. Our attempt here was to demonstrate the numerous possibilities in a typical session that follows this process, step by step.

We all have many psychodramas within us, and one cannot deal with the entire life of the protagonist in any given session. However, whatever is opened and dealt with, must be closed before we move on to the next issue.

The final closure of the session is the *sharing.* At this phase of the session, we have the group move in, physically closer, to join the protagonist and the director. The group is asked to share their own feelings and responses to what they have just experienced in the protagonist's session. The sharing should be structured so that the group members understand it is not a time for analyzing, advice giving, interpreting or questions. Instead, it is a time to give something of themselves. The protagonist has just revealed, through the session, his/her deepest feelings, fears, traumas and experiences. We encourage everyone in the group to share and our team shares with the protagonist when appropriate. Within the bosom of the psychodramatic family, (his students) Moreno often called this part of the session "love-back." The sharing is a part of the healing process for the protagonist. It is the time when the individual discovers that he/she is not alone with those feelings and experiences. It is the time when the protagonist feels the acceptance of the group despite flaws, weaknesses and difficulties. It is a time that reinforces the cohesiveness of the group. In addition to the primary functions of the sharing, there are other advantages to this section of the process. Often new material, previously unrevealed or long forgotten is brought forth. New protagonists are warmed up and emerge for the future. The group becomes supportive of each other, and they become a community.

The fourth, and sometimes optional, part of the session is the *dialogue.* In our hospital setting the dialogue is the time when the director/therapist does any interpretation, analysis or discussion with the protagonist and the group. This is the appropriate time for feed-back. Here each director will use his/her personal form and particular philosophy in using the dialogue. When the director feels the protagonist and/or the group cannot integrate any additional emotion or information, the dialogue should be delayed until another time.

We remind our readers that every session will not move in the exact order described in the prototype. However, when the psychodramatic process is followed, step by step, the session will have meaning and clarity, the essential elements of the therapeutic process. When there is no process and no clarity, one has a chaotic melange of techniques strung together without purpose.

The spiral was developed as an aid to teach students the process of classical psychodrama. However, the concepts we have stated along with the manner of tracking and focusing can be used as a model for group and individual therapy with clients. Whether we are using the action of psychodrama or using traditional therapy with clients, we use the same process as our guide.

Begin with the present problem.
Find the similarities in the recent past.
Discover the linkages to the deep past.
Help the client understand his/her process in life.
Achieve a catharsis, if necessary.
Concretize the issues, choices and actions that keep the client in the present dysfunctional state.
Help him/her to see the options in life.
Aid in the integration of the cognitive and the affective.
Achieve closure and healing so that the client can act out in life what has been learned in therapy.

There is an ordered simplicity in a process that is beyond knowledge of techniques and psychology.

Autonomy, self-determination and dignity are the birthright of every human being. Psychodrama and any sound use of psychotherapy can help individuals to recover that integrity, that adherance to values and wholeness.

Kate Stout writing about the work of Pulitzer Prize playwright, Marsha Norman, states, "that freedom and dignity come from a sense of control over one's life; that faith in oneself is responsible for most of what is accomplished in the world; and that hope is the key to survival."[7]

Notes

1. L. J. Fine, "Psychodrama," *Current Psychotherapies,* Ed. Raymond Corsini, Ph.D., (Itasca, Illinois: F. E. Peacock Publishers, Inc., 1978), p. 15.
2. Suzanne Langer, *Philosophy in a New Key,* (Cambridge: 1942).
3. Ibid.
4. Mihaly Czikszentmihalyi and Eugene Rochberg-Halton, "Object Lessons," *Psychology Today,* (Dec. 1981), p. 79–84.
5. Ibid.
6. Ibid.
7. Kate Stout, "Marsha Norman: Writing for the Least of our Brethren," *Saturday Review,* (Oct. 1983), p. 31.

Section III
Sharing

In this section we will share a variety of patient sessions we have directed over the years. As we describe each session we will track it on the spiral and note our choice points, decisions and thought processes while directing that session.

Preceding this section it is important to note that psychodrama is not a panacea. It is an excellent tool for a wide variety of diagnoses. Psychodrama is used, in our setting, as an integral part of the patient's therapy while hospitalized. During this period the patient is seen regularly by his/her individual psychiatrist and attends other group therapies. In turn, the psychodrama team sees the patient outside of the psychodrama theatre for follow-up, discussion and integration of their psychodrama work. Our team attends patient staffings and reviews; consults with the psychiatrist and other hospital staff regarding the patient's progress.

"Psychodrama and psychoanalysis need not be at odds; rather, both are similar in that they act as root methods . . . both approaches have been modified extensively and have been incorporated into other methods . . . the addition of psychodramatic methods to conventional verbal forms extends the power of psychotherapy. Verbal and non-verbal forms need not be at opposite poles, for it is quite possible to interweave the aspects of cognitive and experiential, objective and subjective, and other polarities of human experience."[1]

Classic Sessions

The sessions described in this book have been written in such a way as to protect the privacy of the individuals and the families involved.

JOHN

This session was somewhat unusual since both the husband and wife were present and involved in the session. The husband was the identified patient and had asked his wife to be present. (It was not technically a double protagonist session because we worked primarily with the husband. However, the wife did play her own role and we did check out the perceptions of her husband.) The protagonist is a thirty-five-year-old blue-collar worker who is hospitalized for severe depression. His presenting problem is his "strained relationship" with his wife of sixteen years. (See Figure C, Page 38)

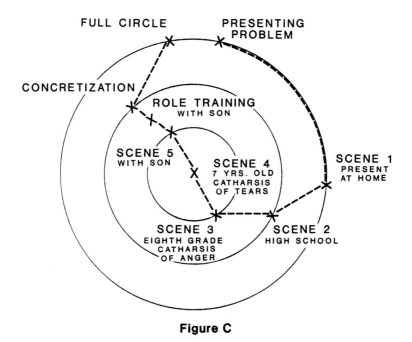

Figure C

They are the parents of one twelve-year-old son, Jimmy. We go to a recent scene where John feels the relationship is strained. (Scene One) It is in their bedroom. Carol is described by John as "strong and outgoing." In this scene, Carol being herself, says, "I can't stand it, all you do is criticize and yell at us and upset Jimmy, or you don't pay any attention to us. You better change it, or it will be too late." During the ultimatum, John becomes extremely angry. He pounds on the bed and he says, "I am sick and tired of these damn inferior feelings; I've felt dumb and stupid all of my life." (Note: Since we know he expresses his anger easily, the cue regarding his inferior feelings is the important one to track. This is a case of inferiority being the process and the anger the content. He feels inferior and then gets angry.)

When asked at what other times in his life he has had these same inferior feelings, John immediately takes us to a time when he was in high school. (Scene Two) He describes his father as a "housepainter with a 'horse shit' personality who drinks." Mother is described as "strong and caring." (Note: The director, realizing that there may be a number of scenes developing, decides to use an action sociogram for the high school scene.) We ask John to place father and mother in space relationship to himself as he perceives the family interaction at this significant point in his life. He places his father and himself literally nose to nose with fists clenched. Meanwhile, mother is placed five feet from both husband and son with her fists also clenched. Father's message to John is, "I am going to make you into something if I have to beat it into you." Mother's message is, "Leave John alone." John's message to father is, "I hate you. I am going to knock your head off." As we have mother and father repeat their messages to John, he becomes extremely angry and we freeze him. (Technically for this director, it is too early to allow him to cathart his anger. We do not yet have enough information nor do we see the total threads of John's present problems.)

John then takes us to another scene, when he is in the eighth grade. (Scene Three) This takes place in the home of an aunt and uncle. Father is seated in the kitchen with the relatives and calls John into the room. He says to the others, "I want to introduce you to the dumbest kid in the whole class." As father repeats his message, John's anger rises. At this point, we allow him to vent his anger. We give him the bataka which he uses vigorously, screaming and finally exhibiting a few tears. He drops to the floor, exhausted, after the catharsis. (We allow him to cathart his anger at this point for two reasons. One, we can now see the threads of humiliation and abasement by father; and second, after having his anger frozen a number of times, the protagonist needs the gratification of releasing that anger.)

The transition to the next scene is facilitated by the cue of John's tears after his catharsis of anger. Therefore, we ask the question, "What other feelings besides anger do you have?" John answers, "Frustration." We now go to a scene when he feels frustration in addition to the anger. (Scene Four) This is when John is seven years old and in the first grade. Present in this scene are John and mother, who is attempting to help him read. John is feeling dumb and frustrated because he is having so much difficulty. Father enters and his message to John is, "I don't know you exist; you are so dumb." At first John is angry, but that very quickly changes to sadness as he says, "I want to help, but Dad just yells." (Note: This is a significant cue since it directly relates to the first scene and the comment of John's wife: "All you do is criticize and yell and upset Jimmy.") As we sense his anger changing to sadness, we give him a "double." With the help of the double, the seven-year-old John begins to cry, saying, "Please love me, please love me." The patient breaks down and cries deeply. (He later tells us that he has not cried or had any tears since he was five years old.)

When the protagonist is calm once more, we ask the key question, "Did you promise yourself as a child that you would be different than your father?" The protagonist immediately agrees and this gives us our transition to the next scene. (Scene Five) We move to John and his son, Jimmy, in the present. John tries to talk to his son, but is unsuccessful. Nor can the son speak to the father. We then role reverse the father and son. As his son, John says, "I am afraid of you because you swear and yell; I'm frustrated and afraid, and I need your love and attention." As we can see, in this most significant role, John understands the feelings of his son, and as noted earlier, they are much like his own feelings with his father. (Since this protagonist was immediately aware of the parallels, it was not necessary to use a mirror to demonstrate the similarities between his father and him.) Back in his own role, he is now finally able to tell his son about himself, his father, and his feelings as a child and as a man. Since the connection has been made that John's behavior with Jimmy is a re-enactment of the pattern set by his own father, John is able to act on his feelings. He says, "I have to show him that it is time to quit the apologies and start the feelings." In this scene, although it is difficult, John is finally able to embrace his son. (Note: This physical movement is a significant part of the session, the role training. John, as a child, and even as an adult, was never taught tenderness, physical touch, and its importance. Because of this, he was unable to transmit them to his own son. By having John do this, even with an auxiliary playing the role of his son, it will enable him to live out these actions in life.)

We then concretize the session. For the concretization, we come back to the present, to the point where John's marriage is crumbling and he, himself, cannot cope with his feelings of depression, anger and fear. (Note: Remember that we must help him see what his contributions are to his present difficulties, and to help him make some decision about how he wants to handle his life.) In the concretization, we bring John's wife back and ask him how far apart he feels they have been during the past eight years. We ask him to do this by using the space in the room, symbolically. John places Carol at the opposite end of the room. We ask him what the space between them represents and he names four issues. As he names them, we have him place a chair to represent each one, between Carol and him. The issues are; Fear of feelings, inability to communicate feelings, fear of being like father, and fear that he cannot change. We explain clearly to John the symbolism of the space and what the chairs represent. We then tell him that as a child, he had no control over his father's actions and/or responses to him. However, he is no longer a child and is responsible for himself and his own actions in the present. When this is clear, we ask him to show us what he would like to do with his life. John begins to dispose of the chairs that separate him from Carol. After he has done this, he moves quickly across the room and embraces his wife. (Note: Since we have done a role training scene with his son, and his wife has been present for the session, it is unnecessary to do another role training scene at this time.)

This session is an excellent example of the necessity to complete the psychodramatic process. For example, some psychodramatists might have ended the session after the catharses of anger and tears. Some may have ended the session right after the scene of reconciliation with the father and son. For us, neither of these segments is the end of the session. As noted, we must go on to concretize John's responsibility for his present choices in life, and thus bring the session full circle to himself in the present.

Although this session was focused primarily on John, it was significant that his wife was present. Previously Carol had not understood the reasons behind John's criticism and coldness. Watching his childhood scenes and seeing him cry had a tremendous emotional impact upon her.

ANN

Ann, age thirty, is protagonist in a session dealing with "her relationship with her husband and her feelings of "powerlessness." (See Figure D Page 43)

We begin with a recent scene between Ann and her husband arguing about power. (Scene One) Alan, her husband of fourteen years, is described as "strong, mentally and physically." The relationship is "shaky and fake most of the fourteen years." Their eleven year old daughter, Melissa, is described as "sensitive and aware, but distant from me. She reminds me of myself, withdrawn and closed off." As Ann describes the child, she bursts into tears. When she is calm, we play out the scene. In this scene Alan says, "You have all the power over me and have reduced me to nothing. You have never loved me and that has made me feel cheated." Ann feels "guilty" and says, "You are right. I have used you, berated you and I still feel powerless." When asked where else she feels powerless in the present, she says, "At work."

We move to a time and place at work. (Scene Two) We quickly discover that Ann feels she is limited at work and also has "limited power."

We go to another scene at home. (Note: We need to see the dynamics of her relationship with her daughter.) (Scene Three) In a symbolic sociogram with her daughter Melissa, we see that Ann feels that she does not "have the power to reach Melissa." We also see that Melissa is withdrawn and distant.

Since the issue of power has been so significant, we go to another time when Ann has felt she has no power. We ask her to show us a time when it is the worst for her.

She takes us to a time and place when she is fourteen years old. (Scene Four) The scene is in her bedroom at home. (Note: There are no significant objects in her life at this time and we found none in Scenes One and Two. The fact that there are no significant objects in a person's life is also an important cue.) Living in the house are mother, stepfather and four younger brothers and sisters. Ann is a child of the mother, while her brothers and sisters are the biological children of her mother and present step-father. She does not know her own father. Mother is described as "passive and having no power." The relationship is "I'm mother's helper." Step-father is described as "military and cold." We find that Ann ignores him because she wants to avoid him and he avoids her because of guilt. (Note: During the session, we have repeatedly asked Ann to show us with her body the feelings of "guilt,

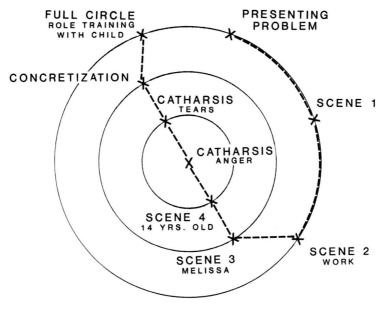

Figure D

powerlessness, etc. . . ." Her rigidity and fear have made this impossible for her to do. Therefore, rather than pressure her, we must discover other ways to enable her to be in touch with her feelings. See Rules and Techniques, Page 10.) In the warm-up to the scene, Ann soliloquizes her fourteen year old feelings. "I don't like school because my friends don't go there and I feel alone. My stepfather is Catholic so I have to go to a parochial school where it feels cold, just like home. I hate everything except when I am outside of the house." In the scene, the fourteen year old Ann is asleep in the middle of the night when she is awakened by a noise at her door. (Note: The director intuited that this was a case of molestation by the step-father. We prepared for this by lowering the lights, cuing the auxiliary playing the role of step-father, creating the noise and having step-father enter the room. This put the protagonist immediately at the time and place so that she was able to respond spontaneously.) Ann is extremely frightened as soon as she hears the door and for the first time uses her body as she curls up into a fetal position. Step-father's main message as he enters the room is, "I'm in control of you." Mother's main message (although she is not in the room) is, "Don't make waves; remember you are my helper." As the molestation takes place, we help Ann to be in touch with the fear and revulsion of this earlier time, as well as the deep anger she has never allowed herself to express. With the help of a double standing very close to her, Ann allows the "withdrawn, closed-off self" to be angry for all the years of abuse. As she swings the bataka on the platform repeatedly, she screams her hate at her step-father. It is only after this catharsis of anger, that Ann's face and body reveal the other emotions she is feeling. She breaks down in tears and allows the director to hold her and comfort her. (Note: Previous to this, she has not allowed anyone to touch her.)

Returning to the present we ask Ann if she wants to continue in the marriage. (Note: This is important to know. We want to help Ann deal with what is real.) She says, "I am unsure. I would like to be close to Melissa to help her to grow and be different than me. I feel I cannot get near her." We ask Ann to show us the symbolic distance that separates them. She places Melissa at the opposite end of the room from her. We ask Ann to place her body in what she considers the position of "powerlessness" and she crosses her arms over her chest and describes it as a shield to protect her.

Using her symbol of powerlessness we concretize the session. We ask her, "What are the parts of you that keep you withdrawn, closed-off and powerless? We make it clear that these are the parts that keep her from life as well as from Melissa. Ann names the following: "I might get hurt if I open up; I failed once. I might fail again; It's too hard so I might give up; I've been a fake before; I might be dishonest again." We ask members of the group who have these same feelings to raise their hands. We choose auxiliaries to be each of the four parts of her "shield." We have those auxiliaries place themselves around Ann and shield her from Melissa. We explain, clearly, that this is her symbol. As a child, she needed the protection and was, indeed, powerless over step-father's strength and mother's indifference. Now, no longer a child, her protection keeps her powerless and away from her child. As she hears Melissa's message, "I need you Mama," Ann breaks through her shield of powerlessness and with tremendous emotion runs across the room. She holds her daughter close and cries softly as she rocks her.

KATHERINE

Katherine is a fourteen-year-old protagonist with a presenting problem of "anger at stepmother and father." (See Figure E, Page 45) We begin with a recent scene when she feels this anger. (Scene One) It is at a family meeting concerning her running away from the hospital rather than facing her problems. The significant object to Katherine is a unicorn necklace given to her by her real mother, who died when Katherine was nine years old. In the scene, the stepmother is described as "bitchy and she yells at me" and our relationship is "crummy." Dad "gets angry at me all the time" and our relationship is "distant." The doctor is described as "quiet and helpful." In the warm-up to the scene, we ask Katherine to put her body in the shape of her anger. She doubles her body over, her arms covering her head. With the help of a double, we discover that her feelings are actually "sad and scared," rather than angry. When we ask her to show us her anger, she remains bent over but with fists clenched. Both positions elicit tears. In the scene, father's main message is, "I don't want you at home." Stepmother's message is, "I don't want to give you anymore chances." Katherine feels, "angry at myself for leaving the hospital, useless, like I can't get myself out of this, and I'm scared that I used my last chance." Through an aside, we

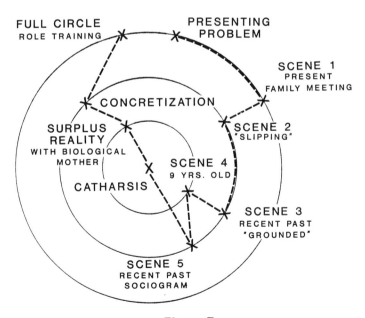

Figure E

learn from Katherine that she entered the hospital because, "I was a truant, using drugs and running away from home for long periods of time." (Note: The director is now aware of several cues that represent the protagonist not facing problems.) Katherine states, "At home, I felt they didn't love me. Now I'm scared about going home and slipping back into the same old ways." Using the concept of fear of "slipping into the old ways" as a transition, we move to the next scene. (Scene Two) We ask her to show us, actionally, how she slips. She begins to move rapidly and in an irregular, frenetic pattern around the room. "I get stoned four or five times a week on pot or speed; I've dropped two classes at school and I don't come home." (Note: While doing this she has had her arms over her head, therefore the director realizes that both her actions and her words indicate not facing things.)

In the next scene, with father and stepmother, Katherine has been grounded for her irresponsibility. (Scene Three) She tells stepmother, "You have no right to tell me what to do; you're not my mother." With the help of a double, she is able to say, "I am angry that Dad married you. I got more attention when you weren't here." When asked, she admits in an aside, "Sometimes I try to split them up. The things I do are just to get back at them."

In order to understand the change in the protagonist, we move to a time when it was different. (Scene Four) Nine-year-old Katherine is now getting all of Dad's attention. She describes her father as "good and happy" and the relationship as "very close," although her mother has died five months earlier. In this scene, we find father, younger sister and Katherine. Katherine shows us how she keeps her anger and sadness in control by feeling important. "I do stuff my mom used to do; I play with my sister and help out." Underneath, Katherine is able to articulate tearfully, "I miss my mom and I'm sad because she's not here. I feel like I'm supposed to be grown up and I don't know what to do." (Confusion about whether she is a child or an adult is common in these situations. The "I don't know what to do" often leads to doing inappropriate "grown up" things.)

We now use an action sociogram to see Katherine's perception of how the family has changed since father's remarriage. (Scene Five) She places stepmother and Dad arm in arm with sister Emily nearby. Katherine places herself some distance away from all of them. Father's main message is, "I don't need you now," and stepmother's main message is, I'm your mother now so don't mention your real mother anymore." As Katherine hears the messages, she clenches her fists and yells, "I don't want to hear. I am mad at mom dying and at you for not letting me talk about her. You're never going to tell me what to do again." Katherine describes her anger as "a knot in my chest." We help to mobilize her anger by emphasizing the pressure in her chest. As she begins to mobilize the anger at mother's death, we hand her a bataka and at the appropriate moment allow her to cathart her anger on the platform. As she does this, a double helps her to make the transition from the anger at mother's death to the anger at herself for her own irresponsible behavior. (This movement clearly shows our philosophical bias that the protagonist assumes responsibility for self.) When the catharsis is complete, Katherine breaks down in tears. We use the tears as a transition to a scene in surplus reality with her biological mother in order to enable Katherine to ask for what she needs.

We ask her to wear the unicorn necklace which mother gave her. (Note: The director has remembered the cue of the original significant object which is connected with real mother and with Katherine's true feelings.) Katherine tells mother how much she misses her and how lost she has been. In the reverse role as mother, Katherine says to herself, "I didn't want to leave you. Remember why I gave you the unicorn necklace. You are very special to me and very loved." Back in her own role, Katherine says, "I don't know how to get along with my stepmother and I'm still angry at Dad." In reverse role as mother, Katherine says, "It has been hard for her to take my place. Would you be willing to try harder with her and with your Dad, and stop doing the things that get you into trouble?" (Note: This is the protagonist in role reversal, giving the "advice.") In her own role Katherine promises mother that she will change. We have her say goodbye to mother in her own way.

We then concretize the total session. We ask Katherine how she would like to be. She describes the Katherine who is "open with her feelings, is close to father and stepmother and who is a responsible person." We have her choose an auxiliary to represent her ideal self and have the auxiliary stand apart from Katherine. We then ask Katherine to place her body in the position of how she has felt about herself these past years. She places herself in a kneeling position with her arms covering her head. (Note: Again the repeated symbol, physically, of not facing her problems.) When asked, she describes the feeling as a "wall" that separates her from whoever she would like to be. We then have her name the parts of her wall that keep her in this position. She names "anger at mother's death, anger at father's remarriage, fear of father's rejection, and fear that I can't live without drugs." We use auxiliaries, from the group, to represent each of the parts of the wall Katherine has identified. (Note: These auxiliaries are chosen by asking which group members have the feelings Katherine has named. As they raise their hands, we choose them to represent the part with which they identify.) The parts of Katherine separate her from her ideal self. We ask her not to speak but to show us in action if she wants to change. We make it clear that this is her symbol and her choice. She finally breaks through her wall with energy and runs to her ideal self. We conclude with a role training exercise so that Katherine can experience self without her wall. We use only Katherine and stepmother so that the focus can be on the most difficult relationship in the family constellation. Katherine says, "I will try to understand how you feel, but I also have a right to think and talk about my real mother." In the reverse role as stepmother, Katherine says, "I will try too. It has been hard for me to be your mother." Back in her own role, Katherine spontaneously hugs her stepmother and allows stepmother to hold her while she cries.

MARIA

Maria is forty-six years old and has been hospitalized for severe depression. The presenting problems are immobilizing fear and constant physical pain. (See Figure F Page 50)

We begin in the present with a recent scene in which Maria is feeling both the intense fear and the pain in her chest. (Scene One) She is alone at home, in the back room of the house, lying on the couch. Although she is alone, she feels the "presence of my husband and daughter." (Although both husband and daughter are not present, we get auxiliaries since the protagonist has already stated that she feels their presence in this room.) She describes daughter Sharon, age twenty, as "an achiever who is troubled by my being sick all the time." Daughter Rita, age twenty-five, "is on drugs." Her husband, Tom, is a recovered alcoholic who "feels lost and defeated and guilty about his drinking." We ask Maria to show us what she is feeling with her body. She curls up into a tight fetal position and from this position verbalizes her feelings. "I am afraid of dying, and of Rita going back on drugs. I feel guilty because I should have done something about this family and I did not. I am sick all the time; I have a tightness in my chest that feels like I am smothering, and I won't be able to breathe any more." (Note: This is the second time we have the cue regarding her chest; therefore, we file this for possible future use.)

Although the auxiliaries are not present in this scene, we have them give their main messages to Maria. Tom says, "I wish you were the alive vibrant woman you used to be, who was full of energy and took care of everything." Sharon and Rita's messages are, "Mother, please get well." As Maria hears the messages, she emphasizes the fetal position saying , "They're making me more fearful." Maria feels this fear in her chest. (Note: Again fear resides in her chest.) We intensify the feelings in her chest by using physical pressure and then ask her to let the feelings in her chest "speak." She shouts, "Leave me alone," several times.

We use this as a transition to a scene four years earlier when Maria has these same feelings. (Scene Two) She shows us a typical scene at home. Tom comes home drunk. This makes Maria feel angry. "I wish he would leave me alone." We have her continue to soliloquize and she says, "I feel so heavy, very tired and I am having trouble with my knees. I can hardly stand up." We ask Maria for an earlier time when things were the worst and she was feeling "heavy, tired, angry and fearful."

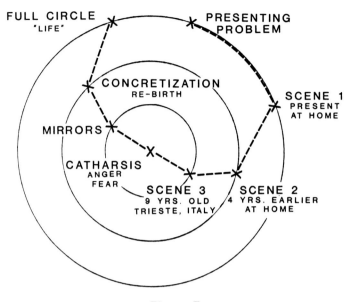

Figure F

We then make a transition back to a time when Maria is nine years old. (Scene Three) The scene is in Trieste, Italy, where Maria lives with her three sisters, mother and father. Father is described as "stern, but he is away a lot helping out during the war." Mother is described as "a very strong, solid woman who takes care of everything." We also learn that Mother is often tired and fearful of the war, but she is still strong. (Note: The director is hearing new parallel cues about mother and daughter.) In this scene, Maria is walking home from school. Mother usually comes to school for her, but is not there today. She describes herself as "a very frightened little girl, who hates to walk home alone." (Note: The director was aware of the bombing of Trieste.) With psychodramatic shock, we recreate war-time Trieste; A barrage of bombs, buildings burning and thunderous noises. Maria begins to run, desperately trying to get home, but she never arrives there. Instead, "someone throws me into a bomb shelter with many screaming people." As an auxiliary lifts her up, and places her into the middle of the screaming people, Maria cries out her fears, "I feel closed in and afraid someone is going to smother me and my chest hurts." (Note: Here is the core of the earlier cues about her chest.) Maria says, "I want to go home, but they won't let me." We intensify the war noises and the flashing of the lights and Maria screams, "Let me go," over and over. This was a deep primal scream ventilating her fear and anger from nine years old to the present. (Catharsis) When she has catharted her fear and her anger, we help her to breathe easily. (She has no difficulty breathing and has no pain.)

We then make a transition to a series of mirrors. (For clarity and intensification, we feel it is important for her to see the mirrors of herself in the early scenes.) First, we mirror the original scene where Maria is alone on her couch in the fetal position, feeling scared and fearful of not being able to breathe. Next, we mirror the scene with Tom drunk, when she is feeling heavy, tired, angry and wanting to be left alone. Finally, we mirror the bomb shelter where she feels closed-in and afraid she will be smothered to death. Upon seeing the three mirrors, Maria is able to make the significant connections and learn that any time something violent or traumatic occurs in her life, "I feel it in my chest, like I am suffocating—just like in Trieste; I retreat into my shelter, only it is me who puts me there. When my knees began to hurt several years ago, it was because of the weight of trying to hold up my family for so long. I learned this strength from Mama, who did the same for us." (Obviously, it is extremely helpful when a protagonist can understand and integrate material this quickly.)

We then return to the first scene where Maria is alone on the couch. This time, however, we help her experience a symbolic rebirth. She begins in the same fetal position. We lower the lights, speak softly to her describing the symbol of the fetal position and encourage her to slowly be reborn. We ask her to come out of the "shelter" where she has hidden and to become the "vital Maria who can dance, swim, laugh, and live." Maria gets in touch with a new lightness in her body and begins to move, pulling members of the group close to her, clapping and breathing deeply as she dances and encourages the group to dance with her in the celebration of the new, living Maria. (Full circle to "life"— the first scene played in a new spontaneous way.) (Note: This woman no longer had any pains in her chest.)

DEAN

Dean, a thirty-seven year old physician, has been hospitalized for deep depression and alcoholism. During the weeks preceding his session, Dean was extremely distant from the other patients. He was unemotional and rigid.

The presenting problem is "low self-worth, loss, failure, anger and helplessness." (See Figure G Page 53) We begin with a recent scene at home with Dean and his girlfriend Eileen. (Scene One) She is described as "warm but evasive." The relationship is "uncertain." The significant object in Dean's house is a handmade crossbow which is a "memento of my experiences in Vietnam." He describes finding it on a Viet Cong and disarming him. "It made me feel safe to have it." (Note: By the manner in which Dean describes this object, we know the Vietnam experience was significant to him.) In the scene Eileen's message is, "I want to end our relationship." Dean feels like a total failure. He says, "I've felt this way about everything in my life. I get no feeling of success from my accomplishments and I can't control anything." (We learn that at times like this, Dean begins to drink heavily.) He works in the Emergency Room of a hospital since he cannot maintain a practice because of his alcoholism. (Note: Since Dean is thirty-seven years old and unmarried, it is important to see at least one other relationship.)

We move to another recent time when Dean is experiencing similar feelings of failure and rejection in a love relationship. (Scene Two) Joan is described as "warm, loving, outgoing and intelligent." Their relationship is "rotten." We discover, as they get closer to talking about marriage, Joan distances herself and begins to go out with someone else. We ask Dean to use the auxiliary being Joan and show their relationship, symbolically in an action sociogram. As Joan walks toward Dean and holds him she says, "I love you." Just as quickly she releases him, and walks away saying, "I don't want you." Dean feels confusion and pain which is buried inside of him. When asked to show us these feelings with his body, Dean says, "I never show them; I wear a suit of armor." With the help of a double, he is able to say, "I must have done something wrong. I don't know what I did, but it's all turning out wrong and I can't control it." (Note: We are now hearing repeated cues. I'm not in control and with feelings buried, I wear a suit of armor.)

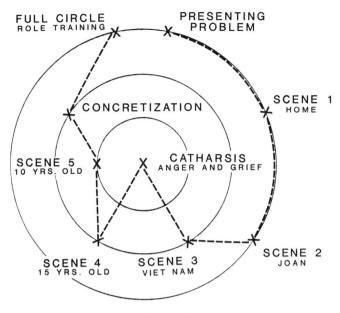

Figure G

We move to an earlier time when Dean feels out of control, but feels responsible for what occurs. He is twenty-three years old and in Vietnam. (Scene Three) Dean is Senior Medical Corpsman of his platoon. He describes the relationship between his men and him as, "The most intense comradeship that I have ever experienced." (Note: As Dean chooses auxiliaries to be the men in his platoon, we are aware of the difficulty he is having in moving to the next scene by the timbre of his voice and his body. The auxiliaries have been instructed that there will be warfare and that they are to fall to the ground.) With psychodramatic shock, we produce the sounds, sights and barrage of jungle warfare. Dean frantically moves from one fallen man to the next, checking pulses and breathing life into them, talking to them and finally leaving their overturned dead bodies alone. Standing in the dim light among his dead platoon, Dean screams, "I was supposed to take care of them, but I can't prevent them from dying. They're all dead." We help Dean vent his feelings of helplessness, loss and rage by throwing metal chairs against the hardwood wall opposite him. (Note: When we have a protagonist with repressed anger at such magnitude, it is clear to the director which catharsis will bring the maximum results. In this case, Dean would have been easily frustrated with the feel and sound of the bataka. Instead, he felt the weight of the metal in his hands and heard

53

the crashing impact of the chairs against the wall.) As the chairs resound again and again against the wall, Dean's anger is finally exhausted. He begins to cry, and he is at last able to grieve for his lost comrades. (Note: He tells us later that he has not cried since he was a small child.)

When he has recovered, we move back to an earlier time when Dean is having feelings of failure. (Scene Four) At age fifteen, Dean describes mother as "congenial but very distant from me." Father is "cold, perfectionistic and domineering" and our relationship is always "strained." We see an action sociogram in which Dean feels "left out, but determined to succeed. Screw them, I can make it on my own." When we ask Dean to show us these feelings with his body, he wraps his arms around himself and tearfully says, "I wear a suit of armor made of pride, which protects me but confines me." Inside, Dean is feeling "loneliness, alienation and no love."

We move to another age when Dean is having the same feelings. (Scene Five) Dean is ten years old and has brought his straight "A" report card home to mother and father. Mother's main message is, "I'm too busy for you." Father's main message is, "You should have accomplished this years ago." Dean feels his anger and says, "There's nothing I can do to please you." The director now asks Dean, "Who else cannot be pleased?" Dean gives us a smile of recognition and is immediately aware that he has been giving himself the same message, "I can't please myself."

In the concretization we ask Dean how he would like to be in life. He says, "To have self-esteem, to risk getting close to people, to not be undermined by what I am powerless over and to accept my own successes." We have Dean select a group member to represent his ideal self. We have him use his symbol of the suit of armor to describe the parts of him that prevent him from realizing his ideal self. He names "perfectionism, low self-worth, fear of intimacy and rejection." We remind him that he is also isolating himself by drinking. Symbolically, Dean deals with taking off his suit of armor and is finally able to say, "I am worth it," as he takes running strides to greet his ideal self.

We then give him the experience of a trust lift since for Dean this means accepting life without a suit of armor. (Role training) Dean's response to the trust lift is, "I am surprised there are so many people who care about me."

MARY

Mary, age sixteen, is hospitalized for attempted suicide and a diagnosis of severe depression. She is an extremely streetwise younster, tough and hardened on the exterior.

The presenting problem is her "hurt and anger." (See Figure H Page 62) We begin in a recent scene with Mary, her mother and a social worker. The meeting is to discuss Mary's return home after hospitalization. (Scene One) Mother is described as "mean and loving." The relationship is "distant." Mary adds, "But we were close when I was little." The social worker is described as "mean and always on mother's side." We discover that Mary's parents have been divorced for two years. The social worker's message to Mary is, "You are not trying hard enough." (Photo #1) Mother concurs with the social worker and Mary becomes angry. Mary, in the reverse role as mother, says to herself, "If you come home you have to live by the ground rules, no drugs, home by curfew, clean your room daily and find a job." (Photo #2)

Photo #1

Photo #2

The auxiliary back in the role of mother, now gives Mary the "rules." (Photo # 3) At first Mary acts tough and hostile. Then with the help of a double, she is able to express her true feelings. "I'm scared of doing this all of my life, and of being irresponsible. I'm scared of screwing up again and mom not taking me back." (Photo #4) We make a transition to the last time Mary "screwed up." (Note: It is necessary to see and understand her process.)

She takes us to a time before her hospitalization. (Scene Two) She says, "I do so many bad things." We have her symbolically act out what she does. The "things" are: getting drunk and running away to a boy friend; getting angry at boy friend and breaking his things; then acting crazy." Mary moves around the room with her fists clenched. She picks up articles and throws them around the room. (Photo #5) She, indeed, acts crazy and concludes the demonstration by pulling her hair in frustration. She says, "My friends see me acting crazy and they kick me out." We allow her to stand alone in the dimly lit room, with her anger and her frustration. As she becomes aware of what she has done, her affect begins to change and she verbalizes her deepest feelings.

Photo #3

Photo #4

Photo #5

"I feel hurt and lonely and I am really afraid of being alone. It's been this way since I was fourteen years old. Before then things were different." (Photo #6) (Note: We know from the early information that Mary's parents were divorced when she was fourteen which was crucial for this protagonist.)

We make a transition to a time when life is different for Mary. She is twelve years old and her parents are together. (Scene Three) The scene is in the school auditiorium. Mary is a straight "A" student and is being awarded a prize. Her parents are in the audience. Father is described as "loving and strong" and we "share everything." Mother is described as "very sweet" and she and Mary are "inseparable." Her parents express their pride and Mary is exhuberant. (Photo #7) The one false note is the description of her parent's relationship. When asked to relay this information, she says, "It's shaky, they act as if they don't even like each other." (Note: It is important for the director to obtain this description since all of the other statements at this time are seemingly "perfect.")

Photo #6

Photo #7

We move to an action sociogram to see how the family is changed after the important happier time. In the sociogram Mary is between mother and father. (Scene Four) Mother's message to Mary is "I want you to stay with me." Father's message is "I'll take care of you, stay with me." As the auxiliaries repeat their messages, fourteen year old Mary becomes very upset. She shouts, "stop, please stop," as she places hands over her ears, refusing to listen to them. (Photo #8) Mary's mother retains custody after the divorce. With the help of a double, Mary is able to express her real feelings about the divorce. She says, "I am so mad at mother for leaving father!" (Photo #9) (Note: this is a natural transition for us to see how she expresses her anger to mother.)

Photo #8

Photo #9

We ask Mary to portray how she has expressed her anger to mother the past two years. She runs frantically around the room pantomiming her actions in a variety of ways. She says, "I run away when mom sets rules, I drink and act crazy and my friends throw me out." She finally says, "It feels like a merry-go-round." (Photo #10)

We then concretize the session. We ask Mary to show us her "merry-go-round" by using chairs to represent each step in her actions. She places six chairs in a circle. They are: "I get angry at mom; I stay out late and rebel; I start drinking and mom lectures me; I take off with guys and drink and drug; I get obnoxious and my friends kick me out; I call mom and go home and start all over again." When she sets out the final chair and describes it, Mary sees the circle, and is astonished. Her affect changes again as she says, "How could I do so many stupid things?" (Photo #11)

Photo #10

Photo #11

We ask Mary how she might be if she were not on a merry-go-round. She says, "I could be calm and happy and whatever I wanted to be. I would be responsible for myself." We explain clearly the symbol she has created. We have her sit in each chair in succession on the merry-go-round. When she is not expecting it, we have auxiliaries move her quickly from chair to chair around the circle. We have Mary name each of the actions as she is moved around the circle a number of times. (Photo #12)

Finally, with a great show of strength and determination, she breaks out of the circle, screaming, "Stop, I don't want to live this way anymore!" (Photo #13)

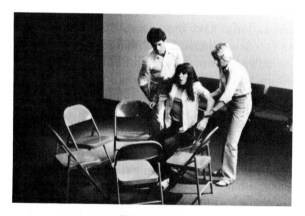

Photo #12

Photo #13

We ask Mary to do whatever she likes with the merry-go-round and she takes each chair representing her negative actions and smashes it to the floor. (Photo #14)

We close the session with a role training scene with her mother. We have the auxiliary being mother come into Mary's vision, but we keep her distant from Mary. When Mary sees her mother she runs across the room, embraces her and says, "I'm so sorry for all of the trouble I caused." As she is held, Mary cries deeply. (Photo #15)

Photo #14

Photo #15

During the sharing Mary says, "I see now that mother was trying to tell me that she cared about me by making rules for me. I really don't want to kill myself now." (Photo #16)

Photo #16

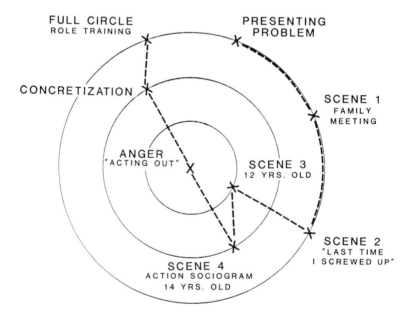

Figure H

There are many nuances in our craft as there are in the work of other directors. All of these variations and subtleties are impossible to describe. We have developed methods of finding an age or a scene, breathing, shifting the focus, using the group, changing the pace and timing of the session and others. These are all due to the spontaneous, creative and intuitive facilities of the director. Each director must use the method of psychodrama via his/her own instrument, self.

Sessions on Death and Dying

In discussing an individual's own death, Elisabeth Kübler-Ross lists five stages in the death process. They are: Denial, Anger, Bargaining, Depression and Acceptance. She notes, ". . . not everyone completes the process. Some people get stuck at one stage . . . some people begin to move toward resolution after a period of time, others move through the five stages relatively smoothly."[2]

Individuals who have lost significant others through death have a similar process. We encounter patients who have not completed the grieving process or who may be stuck at one of the stages. Most often we see patients who are at the stage of depression and have omitted the stage of anger. They may or may not have gone through the stages of denial and bargaining.

Psychodrama is an excellent method for working through the grief process when it has not been completed. The following sessions demonstrate the use of psychodrama with issues of death.

BARBARA

Barbara, age thirty-five, entered the hospital deeply depressed and suicidal. She had become increasingly depressed in the two years since the death of her husband, Robert. The presenting problem is "fear for my daughter." (See Figure I Page 64)

We begin with a recent scene in the car with her daughter. (Scene One) Mary, twelve years old, is described as "beautiful and a good kid." The relationship is "loving." In the scene Barbara is "agitated and worried." She shakes as she drives the car and in the soliloquy says, "What if something happens to me? Mary will be alone." We discover she feels this way because Robert's death occurred in an automobile accident.

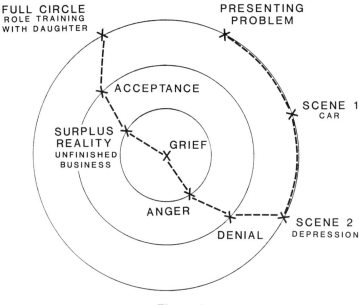

Figure I

We go to a recent scene at home where Barbara is "depressed and fearful." (Scene Two) The significant object in the scene is a picture of Barbara and Robert taken just before the accident. As Barbara describes the picture, she becomes tearful, but quickly swallows her tears. In this scene we discover that she has been ignoring Mary. Barbara's primary feelings are, "I'm hurting Mary and maybe she would be better without me." (Depression) With the help of a double, she expresses her suicidal feelings. Once more, as she begins to cry, she swallows her tears immediately. (Note: The repeated halting of her tears is a possible sign that she has not completed the grieving process.)

We move to the time of Robert's accident and death. When we reproduce the car crash, Barbara screams "No" over and over again. (Denial) We help her to be in touch with the anger which is described as "a burning in my stomach." As we intensify the body feeling, Barbara is able to cathart her anger with a bataka as she screams, "It's not fair," over and over. (Anger) When the catharsis of anger is complete, Barbara is finally able to cry deeply. (Grieving) She says, "I never had a chance to feel anything. I had to keep my act together and be strong."

To help her complete her unfinished business with her husband, we go to a scene in surplus reality with Robert. In her own role Barbara says, "I miss you, I need you, I can't go on without you." In reverse role as Robert she says, "You have to go on. It hurts me when you say that. You have to raise Mary and enjoy life." Back in her own role, Barbara is able to hear his message. Before he goes, she is able to say, "I love you and I will take good care of Mary." She allows herself to cry again. We have her say goodbye to Robert but to symbolically hold on to the "strength that he had." (Acceptance)

We conclude with a brief role training scene with Mary. Barbara is able to hold her child, tell her that she loves her and finally say, "I'm going to start living."

ED

Ed is a forty-five year old amputee, confined to a wheelchair, who has been hospitalized for severe depression. He has been hallucinating his dead child.

The presenting problem is his "guilt over his daughter's death." (See Figure J Page 67)

We move to a recent scene when he has felt the most guilty. (Scene One) It is in the living room of his house where he names the pictures of his three children as the significant objects. We have him choose auxiliaries to be his wife and children. Charlie, age ten, is described as "distant." Jan, age six, is "loving" and "apart" from Ed. Shirley, who would have been nine had she lived, is an "angel, sweet and enduring." His wife, Rita, is described as "warm" and their relationship as "pulled apart." In the warm-up to this scene, we encourage Ed, through the use of his body and movements in the wheelchair, to show us how he is feeling just before the scene. At this moment Ed is hallucinating Shirley and is feeling "a tremendous amount of guilt because I could not save her. It is my fault that she is dead." In the scene, Ed and Rita are discussing putting flowers on the child's grave. Rita tearfully says, "She is gone; please give the living some of your love; the other children and I need your attention." Ed dissolves in tears, saying, "It's my fault and the driver was going too fast." He does not hear his wife's message. We discover quickly that the essence of this scene is that Ed has been inattentive to his wife and children for the past two years, and at the same time, has become more and more depressed as he refuses to accept the reality of his child's death.

We move to the scene where Shirley has been fatally injured by an automobile. (Scene Two) (Note: We purposely do not have Ed choose the auxiliary to be the seventeen year old driver of the automobile, so that we can use psychodramatic shock should we need it. In addition, if we were to stop the action at this point for Ed to choose an auxiliary, we would lose the warm-up to this most crucial scene.) In this scene, Jan and Charlie run home to tell Ed what has happened to Shirley. As Ed approaches the lifeless body of his child, we have the car and driver standing nearby. Ed frantically attempts artificial respiration and feels that everyone is expecting him to save her. Instead of underscoring his guilt at not being able to save Shirley, we help Ed to be in touch with his anger at the driver. We do this by having the auxiliary playing the driver deny that the accident was his fault. As Ed hears the main message, "I wasn't speeding, she ran in front of the car," we help him to

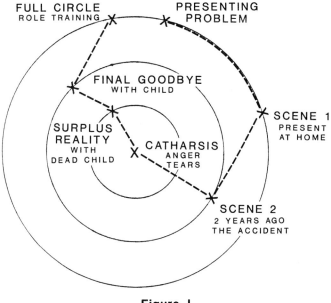

Figure J

locate the anger in his body. He describes it as "heaviness in his shoulders." We have a team member use pressure in that area to help him be in touch with the anger. Finally, from his wheelchair, Ed is able to cathart his anger by beating the bataka on the platform. He yells over and over, "Murderer, murderer." After his catharsis, he is able to release his tears.

We move next to surplus reality so that Ed can complete his unfinished business with his dead child. We have him choose a place that they both love, in the back yard. Ed says, "I love you and I wish I could have you back." In the reverse role, as Shirley, Ed says, "I am with God; it is not your fault. I love you but I don't want you to think of me or 'see me' anymore. I can see you, but you can't see me." The director then instructs Ed, as himself, to ask Shirley what one thing would mean the most to her. Again in the reverse role of Shirley, Ed says, "I want you, Charlie, Jan and Mom to be a family." In his own role, Ed says, "I promise you that I will. I must live for the family and not ignore Charlie and Jan." We ask Ed to say goodby to Shirley in his own way. He holds the child and cries deeply and finally with difficulty says goodby. (Note: We have given instructions to the auxiliary, Shirley, to slowly walk toward the door at the rear of the room, open it, and exit through it.) During this time, the director emphasizes again that Ed is saying goodbye to the hallucinations of the child being alive. We also emphasize that a part of the child will always be with him.

We return full circle to the first scene for role training. The auxiliaries playing the role of the wife and children give their familiar messages to Ed. "We need you and love you." Without hesitation, Ed hears them, and wheels his chair across the room and embraces each family member.

SUSAN

Susan is a forty-five year old woman who has been hospitalized for severe depression. Her presenting problem revolves around her fifteen year old son, Ron, who has a terminal illness. (See Figure K. Page 69)

Susan describes her feelings as a "dark cloud hanging over me." (Depression) We ask her to place her body in the shape of the dark cloud. She clenches her fists and begins to scream, "It feels like I'm going to explode. I can't stand it anymore. I don't want him to die." (Denial) We help her to mobilize and release her anger, physically, with the bataka. She shouts, "It isn't fair," over and over. (Anger) (Note: Although we have cautioned directors not to move to a catharsis too quickly, it is necessary in this case. We are dealing only with the death and grief process, and the protagonist needs the act gratification of expressing the long repressed anger.)

Susan sobs deeply now as she says, "I have been brave for two years. I never know when I wake if he will still be alive." (Grief)

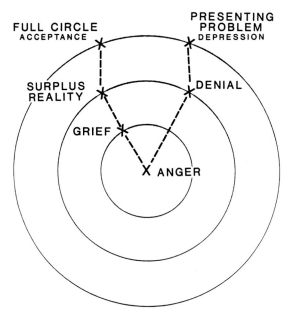

Figure K

We ask Susan where the family shares special time together and she says, "the dinner table." We have her choose auxiliaries to be each of her children and her husband. She describes fourteen year old Jeannie as "warm and understanding." Eighteen year old Frank is "outgoing and easy to be with," and husband is "always there." Ron is "brave and open." When they are all seated at the table, we role reverse Susan into her son, Ron. As Ron, Susan describes herself. "Mom likes to kid and joke and we all depend on her." In her own role, Susan has difficulty and continues to cry. Therefore, we role reverse her into Ron again. As Ron she is able to answer questions about his death. "I know what is going to happen. I've got it together more than you think, Mom." Keeping Susan in the role of Ron, we ask him to leave something of himself with each family member. He gives Jeannie his "sense of humor," Frank his "serious side," father his "heart," and Susan his "bravery." This symbolic ritual concretizes the parts of Ron that will remain with his family after his death. (Surplus reality)

We reverse Susan into her own role and ask her to close her eyes and to feel the love of her family. While her eyes are closed, we remove the auxiliary in the role of Ron. Susan opens her eyes and sees the empty chair. We allow her to sit quietly, feeling the emptiness. When she is ready, she moves to the other family members and allows them to hold her. (Acceptance)

Couples, Families and Multiple Families

The use of role reversal has continued to be the single, unparalleled route to comprehending the "other." Therefore, psychodrama with couples and families, the real people, is an enhancement and an intensification of the psychodramatic process. "Husband and wife, mother and child, are treated as a combine rather than alone, often facing one another and not separate, because separate from one another they may not have any tangible mental ailment. In the course of this approach the family members may reverse roles, double for each other, and in general, serve as each other's auxiliary ego."[3]

We often work with couples in our regular hospital sessions. Following is a "double protagonist session." In this session it was necessary to deal with this couple together, individually and then to bring them together once again. (Note: The double dotted lines on Figure L indicate the movement of protagonist number two, Bill.)

JANE AND BILL
Double Protagonist Session

Jane, twenty-seven years old, is the identified patient and her husband, Bill, is present. We begin with her presenting problem which is "no self-worth, anger, hurt, and marital stress." (Figure L. Page 72)

We go to a recent scene at home prior to Jane's hospitalization. (Scene One) Jane describes her children: Mary, five years old; Bobby, four years old; Jan, two years old; and Joey, one year old, as "intelligent and happy children. I have a good relationship with them except for Bobby. He wants my love, but I can't give it to him." Bill is described as "perfect, and he never makes mistakes, but I do. Our relationship at this time is shaky because I'm closed off." Present in the scene are Pat and Jim, "married friends I met at my church." Jane puts her body in the shape of her feelings, "hurt and ugly." She says, "Bill doesn't accept me, and I haven't been good enough for the duration of our marriage." Pat's message is, "You're not trying hard enough to be a good wife. I did it, and so can you." Jim's main message is, "You are a slut, just like Pat." Bill's main message is, "You are going to do what I tell you. Be a good wife and a good mother. I don't care about what you want." Jane feels, "anger, hate and hurt. I feel rejected and unwanted. I feel dirty. I have always felt this way." The director asks, "How long?" Jane immediately answers, "Fifteen or twenty years." (Note: The di-

71

rector now knows that this feeling has existed long before the marriage.)

We now go to a recent time which reveals the marital dynamics. (Scene Two) Jane is waiting for Bill to come home from work. She says, "I haven't accomplished anything all day because I am not good enough to be in this house or take care of the kids. I haven't done any of the things Bill asked me to do. He just wants to show me who is boss, and I feel like he is the master and I am the slave." (Note: This is the sort of symbol that the director files for future use.) Jane's back is turned to Bill as he comes home and asks her, "Did you take care of the chores I asked you to do? What did you do today?" Jane tells him, "I did nothing. I don't care; you do them." Bill is angry and Jane feels, "He is just showing his power over me." With the help of a double, Jane realizes, "I show my husband my anger by not doing a damn thing. That's the only way I have power." Her fists are clenched as she shouts, "I hate you. I hate what you represent, master and slave." (Note: The repeated symbol.) The director asks, "Who else was the master?" Jane immediately says, "My father."

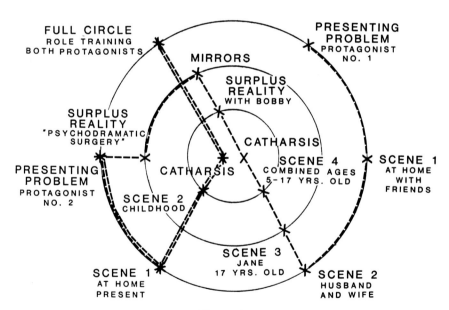

Figure L

We use this as a transition and move back in time to age seventeen and the scene in Jane's family of origin. This is when she was experiencing similar feelings of "master and slave." (Scene Three) Jane is the eldest of seven children. Mother is, "compassionate and a giver. I love her, but I am not sure she loves me because she lets my father do things that hurt me." Father is described as, "a liar and a user. He uses me, he has been molesting me since I was five years old." At age seventeen Jane feels like, "the family trouble-maker although I don't cause trouble, but I get blamed for everything." Mother's main message is, "Don't be a rebel and don't make waves." Father's main message is, "You do what I tell you to do." Jane is molested and then beaten by father until she is unconscious. We then go to a scene where we combine all of the ages between five and seventeen. (Scene Four) In this scene Jane tells mother about what father is doing and says to mother, "Please help me." Mother's message is, "Don't make waves." Jane then goes to the church for help. She is told, "We spoke to your father. Nothing is wrong; just go back home." During this scene, Jane is only aware of her feelings of hurt. With the help of a double, she gets in touch with the underlying anger. We help her locate the anger in her body, which feels like, "something is stuck in my neck and my vertebrae and won't move." Initially, Jane has difficulty releasing her anger at the molestation and abuse, "because I was taught to honor my parents." She eventually is able to vent her anger by screaming deeply, after which she releases her tears.

The director clarifies to Jane that her process, the anger, is presently carried over into her home life and causes hate and power struggles between Bill and her. (Note: The director also realizes that there is a connection with the child, Bobby, to the guilt.) Using surplus reality, we bring in Bobby who gives Jane the message, "I need you Mom." Jane is tearful and pushes her son away. We then show her a mirror of herself in her family of origin. (The time is when Jane asks her mother to help her regarding father's abuse. As mother ignores her, Jane shows her "hurt.") We then show her a second mirror of herself with Bobby, and she exclaims, "That looks like my mother and me, but I don't want to commit incest like my father did. My mother told me I'm just like father, so I can't get too close to him."

The director reality tests with Jane the validity of her mother's perception, and Jane learns that she doesn't have to be like her father. She indeed knows the difference between parental and incestual love. Jane then sees a mirror of her father touching her and giving her the message, "You do what I say." Jane has felt, "too dirty to touch my son, but it was my father who was dirty, not me, even though he has been telling me that I am dirty."

Using surplus reality, we help perform psychodramatic surgery and ask Jane to take out the old tape in her head with the message, "you are dirty." At this point in the session, we ask Bill to participate by helping Jane remove the old tapes. He gives her a new tape which says, "You have always been clean, pure and good." Initially Jane is reluctant to take the new tape from Bill because of her guilt. Bill assures her of his acceptance and Jane accepts the tape and cries as she embraces her husband. Jane then sees her son Bobby, and he is giving her the message, "I need you." Jane walks over to him and tightly embraces her son and sheds tears saying, "This feels good."

We then return to the present marital situation which, as we have seen, is a power struggle. (Note: This is the point to focus on protagonist number two, Bill.) We recreate the scene where Bill returns home from work. Bill's presenting problem is, "anger at Jane because she doesn't do anything." The director immediately asks the couple to reverse roles. Jane in the role of Bill, gets in touch with his feelings of "anger and being unloved when his wife doesn't do anything she is asked to do." Bill, in his wife's role, says, "I feel like my husband thinks he is better than I am." The director, using role training, asks the couple to use this awareness of each other by redoing the scene. When Bill asks Jane what she did that day, Jane gets angry. She says, "You are interrogating me. You remind me of my father—he did that daily and I hated it." (Note" This time Jane is aware of how her anger at Bill parallels her anger at her father.) When asked, Bill was not aware of this. The director asks Bill how things were for him in his family of origin. Bill says, "There was no organization. Mother was never at home and was always too busy." The director has Bill recreate his home as a child. (Scene Two of Protagonist Number Two.) We discover that it is, "chaos. The house is always a mess. Nothing is done. Dishes and clothes are all over and the place is a mess." We quickly reproduce the "mess." Bill is in touch with his anger at the mess. We help him to intensify this, and he takes the garbage strewn around the house and throws it away with great anger. After this catharsis, he releases his tears with Jane. Thus, he and Jane clearly learn why he craves order and organization.

The director now has the couple re-play the original scene. (Scene Two of Protagonist Number One.) We have them do this by building upon their acquired insights. This time, Bill embraces Jane, does not ask her questions, and interacts directly with her and with the children by relaxing with them. Jane feels glad that he is home. Bill feels a lot better and part of the family.

The session closes with the couple making one statement about themselves to each other. Jane tells Bill, "I have let the little girl part of me go." Bill tells Jane, "I can let go of my need for regimentation." The couple then embrace. We lower the lights as they hold on to each other and cry together.

Multiple Family Psychodrama and family education have been written into the Long Term Adolescent Program at Phoenix Camelback Hospital. At the appropriate time, during hospitalization, the adolescent and his/her family come to an all-day psychodrama session. They attend with approximately five other families and deal with the following: 1) major family conflicts, 2) major communication problems, 3) dysfunctions within the family system.

The family unit is the most significant social atom for the adolescent. During long term hospitalization, the family ties are usually severed in some way. In many instances this has occurred before hospitalization. Therefore, there is a strong need to re-establish the family connections and to reintegrate the adolescent and the family. In some cases this may be an original integration where family members have never communicated or understood each other.

Toward the conclusion of the adolescent's hospitalization an additional all-day session with families is scheduled to deal with exit testing, re-entry into the family, problem solving and future projections. We also teach Family Systems Education using a system we have devised called, *The Family Network*. It is based on the Adlerian concept of child guidance and Moreno's theories of role playing, role training and sociometry. This system is taught to families experientially using their own problems and situations. Family psychodrama enables each family member to perceive the roles of the others. Since it is group-oriented, families can identify their own family dynamics while experiencing the work of other families.

"There is a tendency for living things to join up, establish linkages, live inside each other, return to earlier arrangements, get along whenever possible. This is the way of the world."[4]

During the Multiple Family Psychodrama sessions we use many individual action techniques in addition to classic psychodrama. Some examples of these follow.

JONES FAMILY
Mother, step-father and twelve year old Jack

The sociometry of this family was evident the moment they entered the psychodrama theatre. Mother and Jack walked in arm in arm with step-father trailing slowly behind. Mother and Jack sat together and step-father sat on the other side of mother, ignoring Jack. Step-father was a blue-collar worker with a gruff appearance. We began their work with Jack, who is the identified patient. He chose a scene at a family meeting where he is arguing with his parents about having smoking privileges. We discover that this is the issue Jack brings up constantly in meetings. With the help of a double, Jack admits, "I always do this because I know it will get them angry. I don't feel like I'm a part of this family." We move to another scene where Jack has the same feeling. It happens at home before his hospitalization. Jack has been out "drinking and stealing." When he returns late, step-father is angry and he and Jack get into a physical fight.

We freeze the action and explore the feelings under the anger. In reverse role as step-father, Jack says, "You have lied before, I'm afraid you will get into trouble and I'm worried about you." In his own role step-father says, "I am worried. My father didn't care about me. I want to love you, but it's too hard." We use this as a transition to do some work with step-father, George, as we have mother and Jack sit down and watch.

We move to a time when George is twelve years old. He describes the feeling in his house as "small and crowded. I feel angry because there is no love." Mother is described as "easy-going and busy" and father is described as "powerful and domineering. They fight constantly." In the warm-up to the twelve year old scene, George says, "I'm shy. I hate being rejected; it makes me feel lonely." We move into the scene with mother and father arguing. George becomes angry. We help him to be in touch with his anger and to vent it with the bataka on the platform. When he is finished we ask, "What do you do with your anger as an adult?" He says, "I give my anger to my wife and kids." We then help him to be in touch with the "lonely little boy" inside of him and he cries deeply. (During these scenes with step-father, Jack is in tears.) George says, "If only I had had a different life, I could teach Jack something different." At this point, Jack comes and embraces his step-father who holds him and cries again.

We have the family re-play the first scene, the family meeting. Jack says, "The cigarettes aren't important; I just want your love." Mother says, "I have been protecting Jack and making excuses for him."

For the rest of the day Jack sat next to his step-father and mother sat on the other side of him. George continued to show Jack physical affection.

GREEN FAMILY
Mother, father and sixteen year old son, Robert

Robert is depressed and extremely suicidal. He has been on drugs for fives years and has had no communication with his parents. The theme of this family is, "We don't know each other." Mother says, "I don't know what will make Robert happy." Robert says, "I don't know how they feel about me." Father says, "I don't understand Robert, he is like a roller coaster."

We have the family show us their action sociogram. Mother and father, together, are very distant from Robert. Robert has his back turned, arms crossed over chest and head bent down. Father feels "frustrated, impatient and then I just cut him out." Mother says, "I want to bring Robert closer, but sometimes I want to push him away." Robert's message is, "I feel like I screwed up again."

Using the fact that this family does not know anything about each other, the director chooses to do a sociogram with each of the parents in their family of origin. We begin with father at sixteen years old. In this sociogram we see him distant from his family. His body position is bent over with his arms crossed in front of him. He feels, "tight in my stomach. There is no touching, no love. I'm leaving to join the navy."

We then have mother show her life at sixteen. Mother as a girl is distant from her family. Her body position is bent over, with her arms crossed over her chest. She feels, "no one notices me. No one cares about me. I just want to get away." As Robert views father and mother's sociograms, he says, "That's something I can relate to; it's very familiar." Mother then says, "Robert, I just wanted someone to love me. I want you to love me." Robert, aware that both of his parents have felt the same as he, moves to them, embraces them and cries with them.

Throughout the day, Robert and his parents remain close to each other. Several days later we were informed by the staff of Robert's program that the day had been a breakthrough for Robert and his parents.

SMITH FAMILY
Mother, step-father and fifteen year old boy, Jim

This family began with a typical scene that showed the family interaction. It is near the end of the day and we see how each family member warms up to that time. Father is "anticipating an argument."

Mother is wondering "what problems will there be tonight?" Jim is "girding himself for trouble with step-father."

As father enters the house the sociometry of this family is evident. Mother and Jim are on one side of the kitchen bar, together, and father is on the other side. There is a confrontation and then a fight about chores and housework. Jim lies to father. Father is "frustrated and angry." As step-father and Jim argue, mother gets between them and tries to stop them. We freeze the action and interview the family in this position. Jim says, "I can't be what he expects, so I do the opposite to get back at him." Mother says, "I've been in the middle, between them for years." Father says, "I feel like a failure as a father. I've always felt like I can't do anything right."

We take step-father to a scene when he had the same feelings. He is seventeen years old.

In an action sociogram he places his mother between him and his father. His father's message is, "You never do anything right." His mother's message is, "Keep the peace." The boy feels, "I'm trying, but I can't do anything right."

We show step-father a mirror of his life as a boy and his present life as a parent. He is able to see the parallels in the two families and the ways in which he is emulating his father.

Since step-father has been on the "outside," we ask him to change the present family's sociogram to the way he would like it to be. He places everyone in a circle holding hands. Each family member agrees that they would like the family to be this way. We have each one make a clear statement about what he/she will do to accomplish this. The family then embrace each other.

Often individuals who do not participate actively in the psychodrama sessions achieve something from the day, even when they are resistive. The following remarks illustrate a recent case.

GINA

Gina and her father are group members at an all-day psychodrama session. At the outset, Gina decides to leave. She is very resistive and unconcerned that father has come especially for this day. She says, "He can go back where he came from." We eventually convince her to stay, just for the morning. In the opening warm-up she refuses to share. Her father says, "I don't know what makes her happy or sad." At the end of one family's session, Gina finally shares, "I know that I wanted love." She begins to cry and allows the director to hold her.

At lunch time Gina wants to leave again. This time, however, it does not take much to persuade her to stay. She is able to admit some of her "stubbornness and toughness."

Although Gina continued to be resistive during the day, she crossed the room and embraced her father at the conclusion of the workshop.

Several weeks later Gina stopped us in the dining room and asked, "When are we going to have a family session again? I want to come with my dad."

The illustration above is also indicative of the way we work with other resistive patients. The individual is allowed the autonomy of withholding sharing and/or any involvement at the onset. He/she is then more likely to participate later and on a more significant level. (See Rules and Techniques Page 10).

Psychodrama is an excellent method for helping substance abusers deal with their addiction. The following paper was written, in 1979, at the request of the hospital administration for the validation of psychodrama with alcoholics and substance abusers. This was written in collaboration with Kit Wilson, MSW, currently Chemical Dependency Coordinator, Scottsdale Camelback Hospital. Subsequently, psychodrama was incorporated into the hospital's Substance Abuse Program.

The Treatment of Alcoholism and Substance-Abuse with Psychodrama

Psychodrama is a systematic, structured approach to human growth and development in which action and other techniques are used to provide a therapeutic experience. Psychodrama has been used in the treatment of alcoholism and drug abuse since the early 1940's. The positive attitude of our clients and positive changes they report reinforce our belief that psychodrama is a valuable tool in meeting the specific needs of alcoholics, drug abusers, and their families.

There are a number of reasons supporting the compatibility of psychodrama and substance-abuse treatment.

1. Substance-abusers tend to avoid "today"—living in a past that controls them, or a future that frightens them. The Psychodramatic method takes place in the here and now. It is grounded in the present reality of the client's life. The past and future are explored as a means to understanding today's feelings, attitudes and behavior; and then the client is returned to the present. Personal choice and personal responsibility for change, despite past trauma, are core values in Psychodramatic philosophy.
2. Substance-abusers have elevated psychological defenses that make it possible for them to avoid looking at their problems—they deny, rationalize, intellectualize, promise, excuse and blame. In Psychodrama the client sees and feels the truth of his/her own actions.
3. Substance-abusers have usually suffered spiritual as well as physical and psychological damage. In most cases, there is a conflict of values and behavior. Psychodrama helps in clarifying values.
4. Substance-abusers are often very rigid and over-controlled until they drink or "blow up." Psychodrama stretches human beings by

Reprinted with permission.

focusing on creativity and spontaneity; and participation in a session is, itself, a creative act which actualizes into life.

5. Alcoholics are "state-dependent" in many of their social roles, that is, the chemical must be present in their body in order for them to perform that role. "State-dependent" roles must be relearned in a sober "state." Psychodrama provides the safe, accepting atmosphere of the group for this relearning process and for role-training.

6. Substance-abuse is a family problem, it does not occur in a vacuum. Alcoholism and drug abuse, when treated Psychodramatically, is never viewed as an isolated behavior. Psychodrama is an exciting tool in family treatment where involvement of the significant other is used, either with the family member or with the use of an auxiliary.

7. Vernon Johnson calls Alcoholism the "Feeling Disease." Most substance-abusers have been well defended against their own feelings. As they become sober and begin to feel, they try to hide from this new, often frightening, experience. Psychodrama focuses on feelings, integrated with action and helps identify and clarify human emotions.

8. Substance-abusers tend to be vague and general. In Psychodrama, which is specific, much material is revealed that can be used in other groups and in individual sessions.

9. Dr. Jorges Valles, originator of the B.U.D. (Building Up to a Drink) concept uses Psychodrama as emergency treatment for alcoholics experiencing the physiological/emotional symptoms of B.U.D. Psychodrama siphons off the intense feelings which result in gradual decline in symptoms.

We believe that through Psychodrama they can be helped to choose more wisely, stop drinking, stop abusing, and start living.

Sources

Blume, Sheila, M.D. Central Islip State Hospital, Central Islip, N.Y. *Group Psychotherapy XXL* 241–246, 1968

Johnson, Vernon, *I'll Quit Tomorrow.*

Tierney, Miles, "Psychodramatic Therapy for the Alcoholic." *Sociometry VIII,* 76–78, 1945

Valles, Jorge, M.D. Director, Alcoholic Treatment, V.A. Hospital Houston, Texas

Weiner, Hannah, M.A. "Treating the Alcoholic with Psychodrama" Group Psychotherapy XVIII, 22–49, 1965

Wilson, Kit, M.S.W., Clinical Coordinator, ARCA Northwest Service Center, Glendale, Arizona, Discussion RE: Alcoholics

We have not discussed sociodrama and its many possibilities. However, it is an excellent method for particular situations and settings. The following article illustrates some of the possibilities for this method.

"Sociodrama and Psychodrama with Urban Disadvantaged Youth"

Elaine Goldman, B.A. and Sally Goldman, B.A.
Moreno Institute, Beacon, N.Y.

"Upward Bound" is a program developed by the United States government in conjunction with various colleges and universities throughout the country. It is an educational experience used as a tool to motivate urban disadvantaged youth to attend college or some additional training beyond the high school level. As part of the War on Poverty, administered by the federal Office of Economic Opportunity, Upward Bound attempts to involve the youngster's total environment—their homes, communities, schools, and their biggest deterrent, their own self-confidence.

High school students from poverty backgrounds, mostly in the 10th and 11th grades, are selected by the directors of the Upward Bound projects on the basis of recommendations obtained from teachers, counselors, local anti-poverty agencies, welfare workers, or others who know the student. It is not necessarily the "A" student who is sought, but rather the youth whose ability may be lost to society unless he can be properly motivated. Thus, directors search for teenagers who have been denied the access, the broad vision, and the opportunity to develop their own talents and brains commensurate with their natural potentials.

The program consists of a full-time summer residential phase, during which the students live on the college campus for six to eight weeks, and take courses in English, history, chemistry, math, and reading. This is then followed up with tutoring, counseling, and various activities planned for the students throughout the normal academic school year. Students remain in the program, while attending their regular high schools, until they graduate. The summer directly following high school graduation, the student remains with Upward Bound in a bridge program which prepares him for independent college study and life.

This article originally appeared in *Group Psychotherapy,* Vol. XXI, No. 4, December, 1968. Reprinted by permission.

Colleges and universities with residential facilities run the Upward Bound projects and are staffed with both university and high-school teachers, experts with skills in specific fields, and undergraduate students who serve as tutor-counselors. In addition, trained counselors and social workers are employed to help both the students and their families with any individual problems that may arise.

Mundelein College, a Catholic women's college in Chicago, Illinois, which is adminstered by a community of nuns of the B.V.M. order, began their Upward Bound project at the inception of the federal program in the summer of 1966, and each year since, has worked with a group of 55 disadvantaged girls, predominantly Negro, from the inner city of Chicago.

During the first term of the program, there were discipline problems, stealing among the girls, in-group and out-group problems, covert racial conflicts, and other implicit problems that the staff was unable to deal with effectively in their regular one-to-one counseling sessions. The second summer, in an attempt to avoid their destructive operations and to achieve a more cohesive group, the directors hired my assistant and me to conduct psychodrama and sociodrama sessions, in the hope that these methods would help to bridge the gaps needed to prepare these economically, culturally, and educationally disadvantaged teenagers for college and for society. At this time Mundelein College was the only school in the country to add a psychodramatist to their staff and to incorporate psychodrama sessions as a regular part of the program's curriculum both during the summer residential phases as well as in the continuing activities during the school year.

Before beginning work the summer of 1967 an orientation was held for all the staff members. During this orientation various experts in the areas of urban problems, the inner-city youth, and the black student in a white world lectured on the educational, socio-economic, and cultural differences between the Upward Bound student and the typical middle-class high school student. It was through the psychodrama sessions, however, that all participants in the program became acutely aware that the innate human problems that prevent the realization of potentials are the same for everyone, regardless of whether they are black or white, rich or poor, or come from the suburbs or the slums.

Sociodrama and psychodrama were added as a non-academic element into the Upward Bound program in an attempt to help the girls explore some of the problems of growing up, to help them expand their perceptions, and to learn to live creatively.

Our work began slowly as the students and staff were anxious, hesitant, frightened, and some were far from convinced that the method would be effective. We began by gaining the trust of the participants through spontaneity exercises and sociodrama, and the group slowly moved from one of nervousness and hesitancy into one filled with spontaneous and creative individuals.

Three main areas of relationships were worked on that summer, primarily through the method of sociodrama; student-teacher relationships, parent-child relationship, and peer relationships. In the first week of the program, after discovering that a particular class was having discipline problems, we called upon faculty members to play the teachers, and troublesome students to replay their classroom behavior during a sociodrama session. The results of the session were revealing for both sides. In role reversal, the teachers cast as students concluded that "This material is pretty dull," and the students, playing the roles of teachers facing a rebellious class, were terribly frustrated. The session led to an actual confrontation between the students and the teacher in which the issues were brought out and settled. The class was then able to function without further difficulty for the remainder of the summer.

In another session, dealing with the upcoming prospect of meeting a new roommate at college, a student who showed extreme nervousness and fear at having to meet and live with a virtual stranger, handled herself with poise and confidence when faced with the actual situation a week later.

The student's relationships with their parents was another area on which we spent many sessions trying to alleviate some of the problems. Besides the inevitable "generation gap," the Upward Bound students are faced with trying to explain to their parents, most of whom have limited educational backgrounds, what they are learning and why they want so desperately to be able to continue their educational training.

As the program developed through the summer and into the fall, the sessions progressed into personal psychodramas, sensitivity training, concepts of trust and risk, and self-confidence. The work became a two-edged sword and we discovered that we must not only train and motivate these young people toward college and beyond that for a better life, but that each of them must also learn to cope with his immediate local environment—the ghetto, the slum, the fatherless home—as hostile as it is. The students came to learn that things could in fact be changed, and that they could break the seemingly endless cycle into which they had been born.

Although many new girls entered the Upward Bound program in the summer of 1968 there was no difficulty in introducing the newcomers to the method. The summer was spent working further on the ever-present problems of youth: lack of self-confidence, in-group and out-group conflict, fear of meeting new people and new situations, inability to communicate with parents, and trouble in coping with a world involved in a gruesome war overseas, and involved in a great racial turmoil in their own backyards.

It is difficult to present a completely scientific and objective evaluation of the uses of sociodrama and psychodrama with this particular group of Upward Bound students. As mentioned earlier, Mundelein College was the only participating school to use a psychodramatist on the staff. Also, the entire group of girls and staff, including nuns, lay teachers, and counselors, participated in the sessions, so we can make no comparisons between control and experimental groups. Thus, all we can offer is our own observations, those of the staff, and the comments made by the Upward Bound students themselves in terms of the value of these methods in conjunction with the standard Upward Bound program.

Both the students and the staff of the Upward Bound program benefited and gained insights from the sessions. The techniques of psychodrama, such as role reversal and doubling, helped the girls to see the reasons behind their own feelings and behaviors, and to view other peoples feelings in a new light. The sessions enabled both the students and the staff to look at people and situations without the traditional stereotypes as blinders, and to see that their own doubts and fears are not exclusive, but are rather, part of being human.

The use of sociodrama and psychodrama helped to establish the bonds which linked the Upward Bound students to the faculty and the tutor-counselors by instituting a cohesion between the academic phase of the program and the day to day personal living. Staff members reported that the sessions enabled them to better see what was going on inside of the students, and thus helped them to gear their teaching programs more effectively. In a written evaluation of the sessions one staff member said, "The orientation meetings and staff discussions about the girls and their problems were clarified during the psychodrama sessions with an immediacy that cannot be achieved with mere verbal discussion. The sessions touched me deeply and were the best experience I had in the program."

The students were also invited to anonymously comment and evaluate the sessions in terms of both personal feeling and how the group as a unit was affected. Out of this came such statements as:

> "I was helped to find solutions I had never thought of before."
> "I overcame shyness and learned I can communicate with self-confidence."
> "The sessions helped the group get along together."
> "The sessions showed our common problems and helped to work them out."
> "The sessions enabled us to let off steam in a safe way."

Most significant to us, however, were these evaluations given by the program directors:

> Through the sessions many problems were aired early, thus preventing possible serious and destructive occurrences. The sessions allowed the students to break out of old patterns and expectations, and to rework heretofore unsuccessful situations. In addition, the experience helped them to see that the future can be anticipated, planned for, and is not as terrifying as they had previously thought.
>
> The sessions put many of our students in touch with their inner feelings for the first time in their lives. We feel the rare opportunity to participate in a situation where trusting is built into the experence was, in itself, a great contribution.
>
> Since this program is an experiment in interracial living, psychodrama allows each of us to experience the commonality of our humanity, our problems, and our feelings. Not only did we share across racial lines, but also across generation lines, class lines, and roles. This deepended the understanding of each participant, and freed him to be himself and to learn.

At this time, several other Upward Bound projects have already begun to incorporate sociodrama and psychodrama into their regular program, and it is hoped that other colleges and universities will follow suit in the near future. Although the observations and evaluations we have obtained are necessarily subjective, the directors of the program feel that they are impressive enough to warrant both the continued study and use of psychodramatic techniques with urban disadvantaged youth.

Hospital and Institute Experience

The Camelback Hospitals' Western Institute for Psychodrama (CHWI) opened in October, 1974, under the sponsorship of the Camelback Hospital, Phoenix, Arizona. We began our Training sessions by running one Saturday each month, from 9:30 A.M. to 5:30 P.M. As the student interest grew, we progressed to week-ends, holding seminars seven times a year. Within two years we were ready to extend our sessions to six full days, seven times each year. At present each seminar includes a three day practicum with hospitalized patients. This is a significant addition to our program as students are now involved in a clinical setting. They act as auxiliaries in the sessions and process each piece of work with the director and team. Previous to the student's certification, he/she will have directed a number of patient sessions.

Our training and certification consists of three levels. The Psychodrama Assistant, the Associate Director, and the Director. Each student is examined in three different areas: experiential, didactic and personal growth. Students must demonstrate a knowledge of Moreno's theories and the total psychodramatic process. Students are appraised in auxiliary roles and in the role of the director. Individual personal growth is an integral part of our training. We, as therapists, must be able to examine ourselves and change if we are to help the client process his/her change.

We have developed a number of innovations in the training process which have been helpful to us as well as to our students. One of these is a method of co-directing as a learning experience for the neophyte director. The article describing that method is re-printed here.

"Co-Directing:
A Method for Psychodramatist Training"

Elaine Eller Goldman
Delcy Schram Morrison
Thomas G. Schramski

The authors provide a co-directing method which utilizes action principles in training psychodramatists. The co-directing method is described in detail, with specific applications of how the techniques can be employed in training situations. The paper concludes with suggestions for supervision and evaluation of novice psychodramatists.

During the past ten years there has been a creative outpouring of manuscripts on the training of psychodramatists (Blatner, 1970; Hale, 1974; Hollander, 1974; Schramski, 1979; Warner, 1975). Of particular interest to these authors and others are the issues that confound the integration of psychodramatic skills for the novice director. Included among these problems are the novice director's confusion about the use of role reversal, the inability to properly "warm up" the protagonist to the time and place of the role play, lack of selective attention to verbal cues, uncertainty about how to facilitate transitions from one scene to another, and difficulty in continuing to direct a session when a mistake or series of technical errors have been made. These issues become even more critical when student directors make the transition from the forgiving environment of other students-in-training to the practicum of an in-patient or out-patient group.

As a result of experiences at the Western Institute for Psychodrama in Phoenix, Arizona, the authors have developed and refined the use of the co-directing method as a training tool. This paper describes this method, emphasizing specific role-training aspects of becoming a psychodrama director.

Philosophy

Zerka Moreno discusses her preference for a director *tele* relationship with the protagonist over a more analytic, doctoral one:

Once the protagonist senses the director to be genuinely "with him," the director is free to move again into a more objective position, hence he can

This article originally appeared in *Journal of Group Psychotherapy, Psychodrama and Sociometry,* Summer, 1982. Reprinted by permission.

survey the further needs of the protagonist and those of other group members. This delicate balance of the subjective-objective relationship is one of the most crucial *sine qua non* demanded of the director for effective achievement of his task. (1969, p. 215.)

We have found this balance to be a crucial aspect of how a novice director views his or her work with both training and patient groups. Therefore, the ability of the novice director to remain in the session as the primary director is most important.

The co-directing method, emphasizing the continuous involvement in the novice director (ND), was developed when the second author was a student-in-training (Morrison, 1981). She discovered that when she left a session as a ND, her learning was hampered. All of the authors found the styles of approaching the ND to whisper directions or to intervene in a similar, disruptive fashion to be unproductive. Therefore, the trainer-director (TD) began to intervene as a double in order to minimize both disruption of the session and the protagonist's anxiety about the direction of the session. This emphasizes the psychodramatic concept that the double, as an auxiliary ego, is an arm of the director.

Method

Co-directing is a relatively simple and straightforward method. It is introduced to students-in-training as a method that has evolved out of practical experience with NDs who find themselves echoing Gerard Kelly's statement that "the technical model outlined by Moreno appears too complex for direct application" (1977, p. 62). The co-directing model is presented as assistance to the ND, using the TD in the role of double to:

1. Give the ND previous cues that the ND has missed or only partially understood.
2. Explore and obtain information the ND has missed, such as age, nature of relationships and personality characteristics of the auxiliaries.
3. Emphasize or underline key feelings of the protagonist that are critical to the evolution of the psychodrama.
4. Organize the various cues into a theme of the psychodrama, rather than haphazardly pursuing a variety of unrelated cues.

In addition, it has been continually apparent to the authors that a *tele* will develop between the double (TD) and the protagonist, as well as between the director (ND) and the protagonist. Utilizing the rapport with the TD double, the ND or TD can signal a role reversal and the TD will become the director and the ND the double. This enables the ND to observe the more experienced TD and integrate the cues and thematic material presented by the protagonist, while maintaining a *tele* with the protagonist. At an appropriate time, as soon as possible, the ND double (or TD) will again signal and a role reversal again takes place, allowing the ND to once again direct the session. The immediate, post-session results of this strategy for the ND are more sessions completed, increased self-confidence, and less anxiety about the quality of treatment provided to protagonists.

There are a few basic steps (with many variations) to the co-directing process, that are outlined as follows:

Step 1: The TD and a more experinced ND familiar with the co-directing process demonstrate the method. The ND asks or the TD signals to be a double for the protagonist and the ND utilizes the cues that are emphasized by the double (TD)—an emphasis on a particular feeling, thought or behavior that could be critical to the development of the psychodrama. The TD and ND may reverse roles for the purposes of training, but this is not encouraged. It has been our experience that as a ND becomes more skilled, he or she will rely less and less on role reversal with the TD. It is important that the ND be in the director role at the completion of a session, if at all possible.

Step 2: After the session, part of the evaluation centers on the use of the co-directing model. Attention is given to the mechanics of the technique, how the ND integrates the cues of the double (TD), and how it enables the ND to maintain *tele* with the protagonist without inhibiting the spontaneity of the session.

Step 3: Other students are asked to direct psychodrama sessions and use the TD (and eventually other NDs) as co-directing doubles. Role reversal is again encouraged only when necessary, but in preference to the ND halting a session to ask for group assistance.

Step 4: As the students employ the co-directing method, they are asked to evaluate their own work as director and to double with one another to facilitate their own self-monitoring skills and student-to-student *tele*.

As can be seen in these steps, experimentation within a supporting environment is encouraged. The method is beneficial to the protagonist because it offers a back-up of quality assistance while the ND is developing his or her psychodramatic skills. Likewise, it is helpful to the ND who feels that he or she does not have to abdicate the role of director while experiencing difficulty in maintaining the "delicate balance of the subjective-objective relationship." Interestingly, protagonists and directors report a minimal disruption in their *tele,* and in fact often report a deepening of their relationship in the process of role exchange and doubling.

Supervision and Evaluation

A final note has reference to the self-confidence and skill of blossoming directors. We encourage all students, in any supervision session, to evaluate their own work with these methods *before* they ask for feedback from their trainers and student peers. We have found the degree to which students are willing and able to evaluate their own skills to be directly reflective of their ability to understand the psychodramatic process.

We also advocate a systematic approach to learning the co-directing method, as well as other sociometric and psychodramatic techniques. Goldman (1981), Hale (1974), Hollander (1974), Schramski (1979) and others have provided general and specific outlines of ways in which student directors can map their theory and technique in order that they might provide better services to their clientele and more cogent explanations of their work to colleagues.

References

Blatner, H. *Psychodrama, role-playing and action methods.* Beacon, New York: Beacon House, 1970.

Goldman, E. E. The psychodramatic spiral: A model of the psychodramatic process. Unpublished manuscript, Western Institute for Psychodrama, Scottsdale, Arizona, 1981.

Hale, A. E. Warm-up to a sociometric exploration. *Group Psychotherapy and Psychodrama,* 1974, 27, 157–172.

Hollander, C. *A process for psychodrama training: The Hollander psychodrama curve.* Littleton, Colo.: Evergreen Institute Press, 1974.

Kelly, G. R. Training mental health professionals through Psychodramatic techniques: Basic elements. *Group Psychotherapy, Psychodrama and Sociometry,* 1977, *30,* 60–69.

Moreno, Z. T. Practical aspects of psychodrama. *Group Psychotherapy,* 1969, 22, 213–219.

Morrison, D. S. Co-directing with novice directors. Unpublished manuscript, Western Institute for Psychodrama, Scottsdale, Arizona, 1979.

Schramski, T. G. A systematic model of psychodrama. *Group Psychotherapy, Psychodrama and Sociometry,* 1979, *32,* 20–30.

Warner, G. D. *Psychodrama training tips.* Hagerstown, Md.: Maryland Psychodrama Institute, 1975.

Critique and Processing

We believe the critique and processing of the director's session is an important learning experience. Therefore, we have refined our procedure of processing. At the beginning of our seminar we ask all students to take notes during the sessions so that their processing comments will be explicit. Each student should be thinking "as a director" while sitting in the group. If students can begin to pick up cues and make directoral choices while sitting down, the next step is to get up and direct. The students are encouraged to critique and question the trainers as well as their fellow students. This challenges us to validate our choices and decisions and augments the learning process. When we begin the critique, we ask that no one repeat a comment already made. This becomes a cumulative method which still gives the student validation when he/she has noted the same observation.

We ask the director to process his/her own work first. When the neophyte director is aware of the missed cue or mistake before being told, he/she is less likely to repeat that error. When the director has completed the self critique the students begin, starting with the least experienced and moving up the ladder to the trainers. Frequently students have questions for the director and for the trainers. We ask that these questions are specific to a scene and/or a particular dynamic that has occurred so that all the participants are clear about what is being discussed. We use the Socratic method whenever possible which enables the student to process and answer his/her own questions.

The Theatre

The psychodrama theatre in the Phoenix hospital is a room thirty feet wide and thirty feet long with a flat floor. The group surrounds the center of the floor in a semi-circle. The lighting controls are on the right side of the opening of the circle. Since we were limited by the height of the room, it was necessary to improvise a balcony. We solved this by building a platform three feet by three feet with three steps. The top level of the platform is enclosed on three sides by a steel railing which is covered with thick rubberized padding. This foundation sits on rollers which move easily and quietly and can be moved by one person. When there is any weight on it, the rollers lock into place, immobilizing the unit. This structure is used in the same manner Moreno used his second story balcony. It has been a witness box in a courtroom, heaven, a closet, a castle with a moat, a hiding place, an upstairs bedroom, etc. We have found that its size, mobility and accessibility have made it easier to use than a balcony. It is also most expedient in retaining the warm-up when a transition to height is required.

In 1978 the hospital administration began planning a second psychiatric facility. We were actively involved with the architects in the design of the theatre since this new hospital was to house the Camelback Hospitals' Western Institute for Psychodrama. We submitted plans for a modified psychodrama stage for our new theatre. As we began to visualize this stage versus the flat floor, many controversial ideas surfaced. Our protagonists were often fearful and self-conscious. What would it be like to separate them from the group even more by putting them on a different level? Would the patients playing auxiliary roles be self-conscious? Would using the stage change the warm-up of the protagonist? The psychodrama team, staff and patients began on the "same level" and remained that way throughout at the Phoenix Hospital. In a short time we answered these questions and elected to retain our "flat floor" which works best for us in our hospital setting. The new theatre was dedicated on March 25, 1980. The plaque on the wall reads:

The Work in This Psychodrama Theatre
is dedicated to
ZERKA T. MORENO
March 25, 1980

The Psychodrama Team

Our psychodrama team has five members. The director, certified by the American Board of Examiners as a Trainer, Educator and Practitioner; the co-director, certified by the American Board of Examiners as a Practitioner; a psychodramatist, certified by the Camelback Hospitals' Western Institute for Psychodrama; a social worker and a psychodrama intern. In addition, we often have volunteers and psychodrama students to assist us. The size of our team is significant because we have between twenty-five and forty patients in our group. Although this is extremely large, it is successful in this setting with our team concept. The group is large because we include patients from all of the programs in order to create our microcosm of the world. This means patients of all ages, together.

The team is trained to assist whoever is directing the session in whatever way they are needed. They take notes, run the lights, act as auxiliaries and co-direct when necessary. All team members have an awareness of what is happening within the group as well as the protagonist's work.

A significant dimension of our team is that we have become a "psychodramatic family" committed to each other. We are gentle, supportive or tough when needed, and we always attempt to walk into the theatre without any "unfinished business" between us.

Notes

1. Howard A. Blatner, M.D., *Acting-In,* (New York: Springer Publishing Co., Inc., 1973), p. 2–3.
2. Elisabeth Kübler-Ross, *Death The Final Stage of Growth,* (New Jersey: Prentice-Hall, 1975), p. 10.
3. J. L. Moreno, *Group Psychotherapy, a Symposium,* (New York: Beacon House, Inc., 1945), p. 316.
4. Lewis Thomas, *The Lives of a Cell: Notes of a Biology Watcher,* (New York: Bantam Books, 1974), p. 147.

Section IV
Dialogue

In a psychodrama session the dialogue is the final segment. It is the time when the director/therapist gives some interpretation and some feed-back to the protagonist and the group.

As we conclude this book we will remind the reader that psychodrama is an extremely powerful tool. We do not recommend using the method or any of the techniques without being a trained and skilled director. Zerka Moreno has likened psychodrama to a surgeon's scalpel. It can be used to perform a delicate and skillful operation, or it can become a lethal instrument.

The training of a psychodramatist is a long and arduous one. It takes a minimum of two years to achieve the top level of certification, Director. In addition, the psychodrama director should have a knowledge of psychodynamics, personality theory and developmental theory at the very least.

Power and Cautions

There are many cautions regarding the use of psychodrama and many of the individual techniques. First and foremost, it is important to have a *purpose* for using a specific technique. If one uses a technique without some purpose and forethought, it can be dangerous to the protagonist. Some techiques may be too powerful for a particular individual, some may be too esoteric and some too frightening.

One must be aware of the ease with which an individual can be *opened up* using these techniques, as well as the difficulty and necessity in achieving *closure.*

The psychodramatist must be careful not to provide a fantasy happy ending for a session when the reality base is not present.

We have had success with some suicidal patients when we used psychodramatic suicide or a psychodramatic death scene. The power of having the protagonist experience his/her own death can be invaluable toward changing the suicidal ideation. However, having a patient act out the suicide can also underscore the patient's desire to complete this act. Therefore, the director must be certain that the protagonist will make the choice for life rather than death.

When it is appropriate to the protagonist and to the session, we sometimes use the technique of covering the individual with a blanket during the concretization. We would use this only if the protagonist had given us enough cues and symbols regarding "feeling smothered," "suffocated" or something similar. However, this can be dangerous. The protagonist can decide to remain under the blanket—it may feel safe. The protagonist could have a panic attack because of being closed under the blanket. A number of counter-productive events could occur which would then render the session impotent at the very least.

The same cautions hold true in the use of the rope as a prop for a break-out or break-in technique. The rope can be used for a telephone line, a symbol for an umbilical cord, a bond that is difficult to break or actually tying up the protagonist when appropriate. However, to tie up a protagonist who is phobic could be dangerous. Similarly, we have seen people use a break-out technique when there was no purpose, reason or warm-up, and the protagonist had no idea of what was happening or why. We have also seen a break-out technique used with untrained and uncoached auxiliaries being used as symbols. The protagonist is overpowered and has no possible way of breaking out. When using these physical techniques, the auxiliaries must tread a narrow and careful line with each protagonist. There must be enough resistance for the protagonist to work against but not so much that he/she is overcome.

There are scenes that require extreme sensitivity in their enactment. We are faced, daily, with issues like abortion, rape, incest and sexual molestation. In order to accomplish what is necessary for the protagonist and still keep him/her intact, we must use care and discretion. We usually keep the lights dim during the scene and the director remains close to the protagonist. The auxiliaries are instructed to merely touch the protagonist on the arm or shoulder. (When something more is required, the director will signal to the auxiliary.) The timing and skill in these situations is crucial. See Page 43.

In a *judgment scene* or an *advice giving* scene, it is imperative that the protagonist be role reversed into the judge or advice giver for the significant part of the judgment. It is dangerous for the auxiliary playing the role of the judge to speak a pronouncement that is unreal or implausible.

It is not feasible to enumerate all the specific times, places and/or protagonists when the director must exercise caution. The general rule that we have impressed upon our students in all of these intricate situations is: "When in doubt, err on the side of caution."

Ethics

The personal ethics of every therapist is of utmost importance. How one conducts oneself with clients, with colleagues and with the general public has an effect upon the entire profession. We feel the concept of ethics is so significant that we are including here the principles of the Code of Ethics subscribed by the American Society of Group Psychotherapy and Psychodrama. The complete Code and the Procedures for Adjudication are available from the Society.

This Code of Ethics was passed by the Executive Council of the ASGP&P, April, 1981.

Principles

1. Responsibility and Competence
2. Moral and Legal Standards
3. Misrepresentation
4. Public Statements
5. Confidentiality
6. Client Welfare
7. Client Relationship
8. Announcement of Services
9. Interprofessional Relations
10. Remuneration
11. Research precautions
12. Publication Credit
13. Organization Responsibility
14. Promotional Activities

Organizations

The American Society of Group Psychotherapy and Psychodrama

J. L. Moreno, M.D. founded the first professional society in the field, the A.S.G.P.P., in 1941. The Society held its first annual meeting in 1942 at the Sociometric Institute, New York City, and published its first bulletin, Psychodrama and Group Psychotherapy in 1943.

The A.S.G.P.P. is a membership society especially geared to the needs of professionals who want to learn about the latest developments in the field, exchange information, and facilitate the spreading of these methods on the professional level. It is an interdisciplinary society. Its members come from all of the helping professions, psychology, medicine and the social sciences.

Goals: to establish standards for specialists in group psychotherapy, psychodrama, sociometry and allied methods, to increase knowledge about them and to aid and support the exploration of new areas of endeavor in research, practice, teaching and training.[1]

The current President of the Society is Zerka T. Moreno.
Address Correspondence to:

A.S.G.P.P., Stephen F. Wilson, ACSW, Executive Director
116 East 27th Street New York, New York 10016

The American Board of Examiners in Psychodrama, Sociometry and Group Psychotherapy

Established and incorporated as a not-for-profit organization in the District of Columbia in 1975. The Board was founded to serve two basic purposes:

1. To establish, on a national level, professional standards in the fields of psychodrama, sociometry and group psychotherapy.
2. To certify qualified professionals on the basis of these standards. Two levels of certification have been established by the American Board of Examiners:

Practitioner
Trainer, Educator, Practitioner

Applicants must be certified at the Practitioner level before becoming eligible for certification at the Trainer, Educator, Practitioner level.[2]
Address Correspondence to:

Robert Werlin, Ph.D., Executive Secretary, American Board of Examiners, 116 East 27th Street, 11th Floor, New York, New York 10016.

The Federation of Trainers and Training Programs in Psychodrama

Organized in 1976 as a guild of persons and institutions with common professional interests, to facilitate the mutual aid, cooperation and interdependency necessary to achieve the following common goals.

To foster excellence in psychodrama training and education, and to develop professional psychodramatists;

To keep apprised of the current state of the art, and to encourage diversity of applications;

To foster a climate of mutuality to insure a free flow of information and attitudes among members for professional development;

To maintain, augment and assess the relationship with other related professional organizations;

To teach, support and foster program evaluation and research;

To maintain a professional Code of Ethics for members;

To disseminate official information relevant to our profession to the general public.[3]

The current President of the Federation is:

Diana Villaseñor
6391 S. Zenobia Court
Littleton, Colorado 80123

Literature

There are numerous significant aspects of Moreno's triadic concept of Psychodrama, Sociometry and Group Psychotherapy that we have not covered in this book. One of the most important omissions is a clear delineation of Sociometry, which is an important aspect in the training of a psychodramatist.

Moreno's Role Theory, Sociodrama, Personality Theory, Spontaneity testing and other pertinent information can be found in the literature already extant.

It is important for students of psychodrama to read the work of J. L. Moreno and Zerka T. Moreno.

The current issues of the Journal of Group Psychotherapy, Psychodrama and Sociometry, as well as the back issues, are excellent sources.

We highly recommend a sociometry manual. Conducting Clinical Sociometric Explorations: A Manual for Psychodramatists and Sociometrists by Ann E. Hale.

There are a number of monographs by Carl Hollander that are extremely helpful to the neophyte director. They are:

"A Guide to Auxiliary Ego Development"
"A Process for Psychodrama Training: The Hollander Psychodrama Curve"
"Introduction to Sociogram Construction"
"The Warm Up Box"

There is a fairly comprehensive bibliography available entitled, Moreno: The Roots and Branches and Bibliography of Psychodrama, 1972–1980; and Sociometry, 1970–1980. By Jeanine M. Gendron.

Also Bibliography of Psychodrama, compiled by Valerie J. Greer, M.A. and James M. Sacks, Ph.D.

Notes

1. Brochure, American Society of Group Psychotherapy and Psychodrama.
2. Brochure, American Board of Examiners in Psychodrama, Sociometry and Group Psychotherapy.
3. Brochure, Federation of Trainers and Training Programs in Psychodrama.

Glossary of Terms and Techniques

The terms and techniques below are in the literature of Psychodrama and Psychology. They are specifically noted for their applicability to the psychodramatic process. The sources are listed with the following code letters: (D)—American Heritage Dictionary, Houghton-Mifflin Co. 1980; (PG)—A Psychiatric Glossary, American Psychiatric Association, 1980; (PL)—Terms in the lexicon of psychodrama; (A)—Authors.

Act completion   to complete act in psychodrama that has not been completed in life; validates protagonist's emotional experience and sense of active choice. (PL)

Act gratification   allowing protagonist to complete needed act he/she has been unable to fulfill. (PL)

Action   physical movement; the process of doing; (D) part of session. (PL)

Action sociogram   a symbolic presentation of the protagonist's social atom (usually family). People are placed so that space, body, facial expression and messages indicate the dynamics of those individuals at that time. (PL)

Advice giving scene   a scene (usually in surplus reality) where the protagonist asks advice of someone significant. Also see judgment scene. (PL)

Affective   pertaining to or resulting from emotions or feelings rather than thought. (PG)

Aside   the protagnoist voices inner feelings and thoughts to the director. (PL)

Autodrama   session self-directed by the protagonist. (PL)

Axiodrama   use of psychodramatic techniques for issues of religious, ethical and cultural values. (PL)

Bataka   foam rubber bat used primarily in catharsis. (PL)

Behavior disorder   group of behavior patterns that are less severe than psychoses but more resistant to treatment than transient situational disturbances. (PG)

Break-in   can be used during a concretization for someone feeling on the "outside." (PL)

Break-out   can be used in a concretization where the protagonist feels "trapped," or "closed in." (PL)

Breathing   when the protagonist is having difficulty breathing, it is helpful to have the individual take a deep breath through his/her mouth, hold it a moment and then blow breath out slowly through his/her mouth. Do this several times. (A)

Catharsis   purification or purgation of the emotions. i.e., grief, anger, pity, fear. (D) (PL)

Chairs, folding metal   for use in scene setting, delineating space, objects, etc. (PL)

Cognitive   the mental process or faculty; to know. (D)

Concretize   to make concrete, specific or definite. (D)

Countertransference   the psychiatrist's partly unconscious or conscious re-actions to the patient. (PG)

Creativity   to produce or bring about by a new course of action or behavior. (D)

Cues   hints, indicating information perceived. (D) When a cue is missed, the director can pick it up later. Significant cues are generally repeated throughout the session. (PL)

Dance   protagonist may dance scene if appropriate. (PL)

Depression, situational   refers to feelings of sadness, despair and unhappi-ness. Depression may also be a specific diagnosis or component of illness. Slowed thinking and decreased purposeful physical activity accompany the mood change when the term is used diagnostically. (PG)

Director, as temporary double   director can double, momentarily, when nec-essary. It is best to return to the role of director quickly in order to main-tain management of session. (PL)

Director, objectivity of   director walks fine line between feeling with the pro-tagonist and maintaining the objectivity needed to direct session. (PL)

Doubles, types   multiple, for different times, ages, roles; opposing, for use as means to have protagonist express real feelings; oppositional, two doubles, each expressing opposing ideas; special types, p. 17 (PL)

Double protagonist session   session involving two people who are present (often husband and wife). (PL)

Dream presentation   the protagonist is helped to be in the sleep state. While enacting the dream, auxiliary egos take the parts of the dream as people, voices, objects, etc. (PL)

Drinking technique, with alcoholics   in a drinking scene it is sometimes ef-fective to have the protagonist continue drinking (water) until he/she has the same result as when drinking liquor (nausea). (A)

Eating techniques, with obese patients   role reverse protagonist with own mouth; put obesity in chair and have protagonist deal with that part of self; mirror protagonist eating; continuing to open and close mouth of pro-tagonist as in eating. (A)

Echoing   director should echo significant words when protagonist's voice is soft and cannot be heard by group. (PL)

Empathy   insightful awareness, including the meaning and significance of the feelings, emotions and behavior of another person. (PG)

Essence, of scene   possessing a quality in concentrated form. (D)

Exit tests   role playing scenes to prepare individual to return to work, family, home, world, etc. (PL)

Family psychodrama   psychodrama with the real family members present in their own roles. (PL)

Freeze   director can use term "freeze" when; director wants to stop the action; protagonist is too angry, protagonist might harm self or others, director needs control of the situation. (PL)

Future projection   protagonist chooses time in future to enact; situation protagonist fears, scene protagonist hopes will occur, scene protagonist needs to "practice." (PL)

Goodbye, to significant other or to parts of self   director can help effect completion of "unfinished business" with goodbyes. (PL)

Group cohesion   act or process of group becoming a unit, supportive of each other, honest with each other, etc. (PL)

Group conflicts   intra-group conflicts that can be resolved through use of psychodramatic techniques. (PL)

Group size   dependent on; type of clients, time and space restraints, director/therapist's choice, number of trained staff vis-a-vis patients. (A)

Guided imagery   variety of warm-ups and techniques with many possible themes. Director can have group or protagonist imagine; journeys of all types, cocoon and emergence, journey through one's body, re-birth, fantasy journey, etc. (PL)

Hallucinations   affections of imaginary perception, auditory and/or visual. (D)

Hand signals   director should establish hand signals with auxiliary egos to indicate when to; talk, stop talking, talk louder, turn away, come closer, etc. (PL)

Hardwood Walls   helpful to have back wall in theatre made of hard surface for occasional specific catharsis of anger. (PL)

High chair, or platform   auxiliary may be elevated to help indicate superiority; protagonist may be elevated to aid in dealing with authority figure. (PL)

Histrionics   deliberate show of emotions for effect. (D) Histrionic protagonist requires restraint. (PL)

Homicidal patient   director must use caution and not role train protagonist for reality of act. Director should use role training for increased control. (PL)

Humor   when appropriate, director can inject humor into session. Laughter can be healing. (PL)

Ideal self   used primarily in concretization for positive parts of protagonist; used to create "new" self. (PL)

Idealized, parent child, mate   when appropriate, director can produce auxiliary to be one of the above. (PL)

Insight the power or act of seeing into a situation. (D)

In-situ actual location of enactment, i.e., family therapy in home of family. (PL)

Integration coordination of mental processes into a normal effective personality. (D)

Intensification of feeling can be done by; locating feeling in body, putting body in shape of feeling, echoing or repeating verbalization of feeling, repeating "main message," etc. (PL), (A)

Interpersonal between or among individuals. (D)

Intrapersonal in, within or inside of the individual. (D)

Judgment scene used when; protagonist has been judging self, protagonist has felt "judged," protagonist feels "guilty," protagonist will, indeed, appear before a judge. Protagonist becomes judge to judge self. (PL)

Kleenex over mouth used by director, paradoxically, when protagonist needs specific prodding to express self. (PL)

Language protagonist should speak in native tongue for; scene with other who only speaks protagonist's language, emotional scenes, if language is barrier, show what happens non-verbally. (PL)

Letter technique protagonist writes letter to significant other; protagonist reads letter received or wished for. Can be used during session as a warm-up or a closure. (PL)

Life line session that may require a prolonged exploration of protagonist's entire life. (PL)

Lights, stage four colors on basis of theatre lighting. Red and amber are hot, blue and green are cool. Lights on a dimmer control are effective for; focus on the action, setting the mood, setting the time, giving the protagonist some privacy when needed. (PL)

Linkage a system of interconnecting elements. (D)

Manic depressive commonly called bipolar disorder. A major affective disorder in which there are episodes of both mania and depression. (PG)

Metaphor a figure of speech in which a word or phrase literally denoting one kind of object or idea is used in place of another to suggest likeness or analogy between them. (D)

Mirror the auxiliary repeats, in action, the event(s) the protagonist has produced. The protagonist watches the mirror to see a reflection of "self," or "family," or "how much like father," etc. (PL)

Monodrama protagonist plays all roles—without use of auxiliary egos. (PL)

Moving "feelings" in body i.e., anger in stomach to anger in fists, tears in heart to tears in eyes. (A)

Non-verbal communication director needs awareness of; protagonist's body position, movements, hands, timbre of voice, facial expression. (PL)

Non-verbal psychodrama possible for protagonist to; pantomime session, dance session. (PL)

Non-verbal sharing   when group is responding with extreme emotion, non-verbal sharing can replace the traditional sharing. (PL)

Pandora's Box   the box sent with Pandora which she was forbidden to open. When opened out of curiosity, a swarm of evils was loosed. (D)

Paradoxical intent   something with seemingly contradictory qualities or phrases. (D)

Perception   any insight, intuition, or knowledge gained by perceiving. (D)

Personification   of; animals, parts of body, objects. Protagonist takes the role of any of the above when appropriate. (PL)

Present tense   all scenes should be enacted in the present tense—here and now. (PL)

Presenting problem   whatever feeling, issue, concern, relationship the protagonist presents. (PL)

Primal scream   a deep primitive scream previously unexpressed, which comes as a catharsis. (PL)

Processing   discussion or critique of the students work as director and/or auxiliary by the trainers and group. (PL)

Props   simple objects used in psychodrama theatre: folding metal chairs for scene setting, pads, cushions for beds, bataka for catharsis of anger, rope, kleenex, blanket, rocking chair. (PL)

Prototype   an original form that serves as a model; a typical example. (D)

Psychodance   session done with protagonist dancing feelings and emotions. (PL)

Psychodrama—a-deux   session done with protagonist and director only. Director plays some auxiliary roles, doubles and directs. (PL)

Psychodramatic baby   when appropriate, director can produce fantasy child for protagonist who; wanted child, did not have one, lost child or children, aborted child, has fear of malformed child, lost child to death. Structure; 1) let child be born, 2) let protagonist see child at intervals (ages). With emotional need satisfied, protagonist can be more accepting of real children or of not having child. (PL)

Psychodramatic roles   Mother, Father, Heroes, etc. (PL)

Psychodramatic shock   presentation of a situation to a protagonist when he/she is unaware that it is approaching. (PL)

Psychodramatic surgery   pantomiming of surgical procedure to; remove old tapes, remove suit of armour, etc.; remove characteristics not wanted. (A)

Psychosis   a major mental disorder of organic or emotional origin in which a person's ability to think, respond emotionally, remember, communicate, interpret reality, and behave appropriately is sufficiently impaired so as to interfere grossly with the capacity to meet the ordinary demands of life. (PG)

Psychosomatic   the constant and inseparable interaction of the psyche (mind) and the soma (body). Most commonly used to refer to illnesses in which the manifestations are primarily physical with at least a partial emotional etiology. (PG)

Re-birth director has protagonist go through psychodramatic rebirth, starting with fetal position and slowly emerging reborn. (PL)

Returning lost part of self director (or group member) can return lost part of self (confidence, pride, hope, etc.) to protagonist in pantomime. (A)

Rocking chair, prop used for; act gratification, ideal parent, parenting own child. (PL)

Role model a person or character who models behavior for others. (D)

Role playing sub-strata of psychodrama and sociodrama. By itself, used for; resolving problems, finding alternative, decision making, training in leadership and human relations skills, etc. (PL)

Role repertoire variety of roles individual is capable of playing. Director and auxiliary egos should build extensive role repetoire for; flexibility in different situations, deeper understanding of others, ability to identify with wide variety of roles other than one's own. i.e. social roles, cultural roles, socio-economic roles, professional roles, etc. (PL)

Role training re-enacting an old scene or a new scene where the protagonist practices "change". Structure: 1. choose behavior that needs changing. 2. recent scene where that change is needed. 3. play scene "old" way. 4. re-enact scene "new" way. Protagonist may need to try several alternative ways of changing. (PL)

Rope as prop used symbolically in session, i.e. "tie that binds" umbilical cord, telephone wire. (A)

Schizophrenia a large group of disorders, usually of psychotic proportion, manifested by characteristic disturbances of language and communication, thought, perception, affect, and behavior which last longer than six months. (PG)

Sensibility the ability to feel or perceive; mental or emotional responsiveness toward something. (D)

Sign a fundamental linguistic unit that designates an object. (D)

Significant other presentation protagonist can be role reversed into other to present self. (PL)

Social atom the significant others who relate to any individual (usually family). (PL)

Sociodrama group centered form of psychodramatic action. It's aim is to clarify and resolve group themes, i.e., teacher and student; boss and employee; parents and children, etc. The people enacting roles are representations of those roles, rather than self in role. (PL)

Sociodramatic roles i.e. parent, teacher, virtue, characteristic, etc. (PL)

Sociogram the sociometric diagram of the interpersonal relationships within a group. (PL)

Sociometry the science of measuring interpersonal social relationships and the actions and interactions within a group. (PL)

Soliloquy   the verbalization, by the protagonist of his/her inner feelings and thoughts. (PL)

Spontaneity training   practicing and/or experimenting with new roles and new situations to expand one's spontaneity. (PL)

Stage   area where psychodrama takes place. (PL) also see Moreno's stage. p. 27.

Status nascendi   a time when it was "different." Director has protagonist return to initial encounter. (PL)

Structured warm-ups   warm-ups for the emergence of protagonist. i.e. empty chair, magic shop, photograph, etc. (PL)

Surplus reality   more than reality; extra dimensions of time, place, people, objects, etc. (PL)

Symbol   something that stands for or suggests something else by reason of relationship or association. (D)

Sympathy   a feeling or capacity for sharing in the interests and concerns of another. (PG)

Tabula rasa   a smooth or erased tablet. The mind in its primary empty state before receiving outside impressions. (D)

Team   a group organized to work together. Director; trained auxiliaries. (D)

Technique(s)   a method of accomplishing a desired aim. (D)

Theatre of Spontaneity   theatre J. L. Moreno developed in Vienna, 1921; beginnings of method of psychodrama. (PL)

Timing   the director's timing is important in terms of; scenes, transition, psychodramatic shock, catharsis, closure. (PL)

Transference   the unconscious assignment to others of feelings and attitudes that were originally associated with important figures (parents, siblings, etc.) in one's early life. (PG)

Trust lift   Protagonist on back on floor, as relaxed as possible with eyes closed. 1) invite group to come and stand around him/her; 2) ask group to show non-verbally their feelings for protagonist; 3) have group slowly lift protagonist to approximately their chest height. Help protagonist to accept this; 4) gently, group rocks protagonist back and forth for a few minutes; 5) have group slowly, gently lower protagonist to floor; 6) group should give non-verbal message and leave; 7) director moves to protagonist, has him/her slowly rise and asks feelings. (PL)

Typical scene   if protagonist cannot produce specific scene, he/she should be asked for a "typcial scene." i.e. between protagonist and father; protagonist and wife; with family, etc. (PL)

Unfinished business   whatever the protagonist has not completed in life. i.e. message to significant other, grief, anger, goodbye, etc. (PL)

Unspoken lines   director asks protagonist to say what is not said in scene. This is often more significant than what is said. (PL)

Vignette   short piece of psychodramatic work. Can be: complete with warm-up, action and sharing; unfinished business; grief work, etc. (PL)

Warm-ups, structured

Calendar warm-up: 1. visualize calendar with pages coming off in reverse order. 2. stop when you reach particular date. 3. re-enact the significance of that date. (PL)

Crib scene: (Doris Twitchell Allen) 1. group members asume positions of infants in cribs. 2. director (and helpers) become nurturing mothers talking to babies. "The baby is sleeping, Mother will be right back." 3. Mothers pat the babies, make sure they are covered, etc. Repeat steps two and three several times. 4. the director indicates that it is time for the baby to waken and director encourages "babies" to slowly wake. 5. when everyone is up, group discusses feelings as "baby." This often produces a protagonist, i.e. the individual who was not nurtured as a child, the individual who has lost a parent or a child.

Dinner Table: warm-up: have group member re-produce dinner table with family. (present family or family of origin; or both). 2. see interaction at dinner table. Use material that surfaces for a protagonist centered session or a series of vignettes with several protagonists. (A)

Empty chair warm-up protagonist to emerge from group
Structure: 1. place empty chair in front of group and invite them to focus on chair. 2. to visualize someone in chair—someone in own life with whom they have "unfinished business." 3. it can be someone; in past, present, no longer alive, self. 4. give group a few moments, then ask, "who is in the chair for you." 5. choose someone to "show" individual in empty chair. 6. get descriptions (as in any scene) and then have person say what they have not said in life. 7. director can role reverse, use double, interview in either role, use aside, etc. When individual is warmed-up, director asks if he/she would like to continue working. If answer is no, it is essential to close whatever has been opened in the empty chair. If individual agrees to work, he/she becomes the protagonist in a full session. The director may do several empty chairs before a protagonist emerges. (PL)

Empty chair variations director can ask group to put; part of self in chair, put strongest feeling in chair, etc. When beginning on-going group, (approximately six to ten people) doing an empty chair with each group member will warm-up group to psychodrama and to each other. This also gives director information regarding group members. (PL)

Magic shop a fantasy technique designed as warm-up.
Structure: Magic shopkeeper sets up special shop where only abstract qualities are traded for specific personal qualities of the individual. The shopkeeper can bargain, deny a trade or agree to a trade. The director can develop any creative fantasy shop or approach. The technique becomes an evaluative tool in addition to a warm-up. We generally use it for a group closure, using the known information regarding the group members in order to effect a trade. (PL)

Mask shop   a fantasy technique.

Structure: establish shop and mask as "good." 1. invite group members to come in and look for a mask. 2. when an individual comes into shop for a mask, have him/her describe it. i.e. "What expression in eyes?" 3. have individual try mask on in front of mirror and respond. 4. have individual take mask off, look in mirror and describe face in mirror. Is it different from mask? How? Director can continue with mask (i.e. "Where or with whom do you want to wear mask?") or director may choose protagonist at mirror stage. (PL)

Photograph warm-up   Structure: have group close eyes and visualize a photograph, real or imagined. Each individual must be in his/her photograph. 1. ask for volunteer or choose someone to show photo, actionally, using auxiliary egos for others in photograph, when needed. 2. role reverse individual into camera (place auxiliary in photograph). 3. give camera x-ray vision to see what is really going on in the scene or individual. Director can "see" several photographs and then move to a session with a protagonist. (A)

Willing suspension of disbelief   theatre term indicating ability to suspend disbelief for duration of session. Particularly important for director to achieve this for surplus reality and fantasy technique.

Index